CRACKED EGGS
&
CHICKEN SOUP

Norman Jacobs was born in Hackney in 1947. He went to school in the East End and then to teacher-training college in Norwich and, on leaving that in 1967, went to work at the British Museum, where he stayed for the next thirty-seven years until taking early retirement in 2004.

Norman became well known as a writer on local, family and sports history from the 1970s onwards. His first book on local history, *Clacton in Camera*, was published in 1984, and he has now had a total of twenty-five published, including his own highly regarded childhood memoir, *Pie 'n' Mash & Prefabs* (John Blake, 2015). As well as writing books he has had many articles published in a wide variety of journals and magazines such as *Apollo*, *Local History Magazine*, *Essex Journal*, *Picture Postcard Monthly*, *Speedway Star*, *Vintage Speedway Magazine* and *Cockney Ancestor*. Between 1990 and 2005 he was editor of *Clacton Chronicle*, acclaimed the best local-history journal in the country by *Local History Magazine*. He is also a well-known speaker on a variety of subjects including local history and the Victorian and Edwardian music hall.

He has twice been a district councillor in Chigwell and Tendring, where he became chairman of the Leisure, Heritage and Culture Committee. He has also held a number of positions in other organisations, including chairman of the Museums in Essex Committee and secretary of the Essex Archæological and Historical Congress. He is currently chairman of the Clacton and District Local History Society and chairman of the West Cliff Theatre (Tendring) Trust.

He is widowed with two children, two grandchildren and a cat, and lives in Clacton-on-Sea, where he is a member of the Nomads Leopards table-tennis team.

CRACKED EGGS
&
CHICKEN SOUP

Memories of an East End Childhood
Between the Wars

NORMAN JACOBS

JOHN BLAKE

Published by John Blake Publishing,
3 Bramber Court, 2 Bramber Road,
London W14 9PB, England

www.johnblakebooks.com

www.facebook.com/johnblakebooks ⬛
twitter.com/jblakebooks ⬛

First published in paperback in 2018

ISBN: 978-1-78606-879-8

British Library Cataloguing-in-Publication Data:

A catalogue record for this book is available from the British Library.

Design by www.envydesign.co.uk

Printed and bound in Great Britain by Clays Ltd, St Ives plc

1 3 5 7 9 10 8 6 4 2

Papers used by John Blake Publishing are natural, recyclable products made from wood grown in sustainable forests. The manufacturing processes conform to the environmental regulations of the country of origin.

Every attempt has been made to contact the relevant copyright-holders, but some were unobtainable. We would be grateful if the appropriate people could contact us.

John Blake Publishing is an imprint of Bonnier Publishing
www.bonnierpublishing.com

To the memory of my late wife, Linda.

CONTENTS

ACKNOWLEDGEMENTS

As well as my father I should also like to acknowledge the help I was given by others in bringing his story to life. Firstly, my mum, who wrote down her own life story back in the 1990s and from which I was able to confirm and fill in some details of their early relationship. Secondly, my brother, John, who related a few memories of things Dad had told him over the years. Thirdly, other members of our wider family, especially my Uncle Joe, the only member of the Palmer Street and Boundary Estate Jacobs family still living, now in his ninety-fourth year, and still as alert and active as ever. He was also able to confirm and fill in a few details of life between the wars for the Jacobses. Lastly, David, Bobby, Helen and Brian, my Uncle Davy's children, and David, Uncle Abie's son, who all added a few anecdotes they had heard from their respective fathers.

My thanks to them all.

FOREWORD

BY NORMAN JACOBS

S ome years ago my father, then in his late seventies, decided
to take a nostalgic trip back to the East End of London
from his retirement bungalow in Clacton-on-Sea so that he
could visit, for the last time as it turned out, the places he grew
up in. The visit back in time to the days of his youth brought
back many memories of his young days between the wars. It
seemed to unlock a whole flood of memories that, although
obviously always in the back of his mind somewhere, came
to the fore and for days and weeks afterwards he could talk
of nothing else but the memories his trip had reawakened in
him. I sat there enthralled listening to him talking about those
days, and for the first time I began to understand much more
about what life was like for him and his family in that period
between the two great conflicts of the twentieth century.
Although there is no doubt that the term 'the good old days'

would certainly be a misnomer of monumental proportions, they weren't all bad either and loving families like his made the best of what they had.

In talking about his own life he spoke of things that not only affected him and his family but revealed a large slice of social history concerning the lives of all ordinary working-class people struggling to live in the slums of the East End of London in those pre-Welfare State days, the overcrowded houses with families of anything up to eight children living, as his own had, in just two or three rooms with outside WC and water tap, and the reliance on charity and the soup kitchen for food or families trying to eke out what little income they had by buying stale bread and cracked eggs or other cheap food from the many itinerant street-sellers that came round.

But in the midst of the sheer bloody hard grind of this reality of everyday life, there was the resilience shown, particularly by the children, playing homemade games and making their own entertainment and amusement as best as they could – and probably having just as much fun with a homemade wooden toy or a ball made of screwed-up paper as today's youngsters with their Play Stations and iPads. There were indeed many laughs amongst the tears and deprivation.

In fact, as my father spoke to me, what stood out was the great affection and longing my father had for this period as the 'best days of his life'. As he said to me several times while relating his story he knew no different and thought all families lived like his did. That all families had just two rooms, ate stale bread and went to the soup kitchen. Looking back with the hindsight of history and knowing what we know now, we would quite rightly criticise the harshness of those days, but from the standpoint of someone at the time actually living through them that's not how it seemed at all.

What follows in this book is basically what my father told me in those days and weeks following his nostalgic visit to his roots. As a writer, I wanted to capture his story so people today can learn a little about how families like his lived. As I sat down to write this book, I could hear my father's voice guiding me through it all. His inflection, the odd Yiddisher word and the slang, particularly rhyming slang, were all there and when I demurred about using a slang word maybe, I would hear him saying if it was the right word for the passage I was writing and if it's what he said when he was telling me all this in the first place, I should bloody well use it!

I make no claims that my father's family was anything out of the ordinary for its time and place, but that, I think, is what makes it so important that the story is written down and made available for future generations to understand what life was like for the majority of people in the 1920s and 1930s from someone who was there.

This then, in his own words, is my father Isaac Jacobs's, story . . .

NORMAN JACOBS,
London

PREFACE

I'm an old man these days, living out my retirement in a little council house by the sea. Life is content, I have enough to eat and warm clothes for myself and my wife. It's a funny thing though – often in my dreams now I find myself back in the East End of London of the 1920s and 1930s, and when I wake it takes me a few moments to remember where I am. I have been wondering about the old places – are they still there? Would I recognise the streets and houses any more? So I made up my mind to take a trip down memory lane. And what a trip it was, and what memories it brought back.

So there I was . . . revisiting Petticoat Lane, standing on the corner of Toynbee Street and Commercial Street. And suddenly I was flooded with memories of a little boy, Ikey Jacobs. Instantly Toynbee Street melted into Shepherd Street,

Brune House gave way to the streets I had loved so well as a child. Seventy years started to evaporate and I, being that little boy, was back in my beloved Spitalfields.

Times were hard then, the Great War had not been long over and memories of it were still vivid for the vast majority of people. Poverty lurked in every street, pouncing on this family or that family at its whim. Politicians talked of 'A land fit for heroes to live in', but that was a hollow mockery unless of course you were a rich hero; the poor variety had a hard struggle to survive, most old soldiers we knew were maimed, blind, shell-shocked or just too ill to work. Even the able-bodied found jobs hard to come by after the full employment of the war years and general demobilisation of the armed forces.

We were one of those poverty-stricken families, a Jewish one, living in the East End. There were eight of us children, our dad more out of work than in it, Mum worn ragged, no money to speak of and Mosley's anti-Semitic Blackshirts putting the fear of God into us. Yet somehow we coped through those years of hardship between the wars.

My story as told to me by my parents actually starts even further back in time so let me take you back to 1888, the year the spectre of Jack the Ripper haunted those very same streets of Spitalfields that I was to grow up in and yes, in spite of everything, come to love . . .

ISAAC JACOBS

CHAPTER ONE

JACK THE RIPPER AND JACK JACOBS, 1888–1915

Pulling her black shawl tight around her slender shoulders, Carrie hurried out of the front door of the buildings into the damp, dark East End air. The time was just coming up to midnight on a foggy November night. The mist was swirling around the gas lamp and she could just make out the deadened sound of a horse-drawn hackney carriage clip-clopping along a nearby street. Suddenly out of this eerie atmosphere a tall man, immaculately dressed in morning coat and top hat, appeared as if from nowhere.

'What's a young girl like you doing out on a night like this?' he demanded.

'My mama's in labour. I've got to fetch the midwife.'

'How old are you?'

Carrie puffed herself up and replied, 'Seventeen,' although she was, in fact, just twelve years old.

'I'll walk with you to the midwife,' said the man. 'It's not safe for a young girl to be out alone at night in Whitechapel with Jack the Ripper still at large.'

Carrie shivered. Although she was trying to be brave, she was grateful to the man, and just nodded.

The walk took them along deserted streets through some of the worst, most poorly lit slums in London. Carrie was used to the mud and filth on the ground but several times was startled by strange sounds that in the still of the night conjured up all sorts of terrors for her but which mostly turned out to be stray cats. Suddenly, she heard a rustling just by her foot. As she looked down she saw something move in the dark and realised it was a large black rat which jumped out of a puddle of water and scurried off down the road. Carrie let out a loud scream and turned, throwing her arms round the man for protection. He took her hand and she gripped it tight for the rest of the journey. Somehow Carrie felt completely safe with this man by her side and together they continued their journey with no more incidents. At last they reached the midwife's house. 'We're here,' said Carrie.

'All right,' said the man. 'You'll be safe now.' Carrie let go of his hand and said, 'Thank you.' The man tipped his hat and nodded. Then he said something that made Carrie's blood run cold, 'You be sure to tell your mama when you get back home tonight that Jack the Ripper looked after you and walked you to the midwife.' With that, the man disappeared back into the mist and was gone. Carrie's heart was pounding as she knocked on the door. Was he really Jack the Ripper? He must have been or why would he have said he was? Had she been that close to a gruesome death? But no, the man had been so kind to her and had protected her. It was very confusing.

Her thoughts trailed away as Hetty Solomons, the midwife, opened the door and ushered her in. 'Come in, come in, *bubbeleh*, is it time already?' she said. 'I thought your mama would be ready to drop soon. Just let me get my things together.' Carrie wondered whether she should tell her about the strange man who had escorted her tonight, but decided not to. Very soon they were on their way back.

Several hours later, the midwife delivered Carrie's mother another baby girl, the tenth child born to Isaac and Clara Levy. The date was 23 November 1888 and that baby was my mother, Rebecca Levy.

She was born in what were called the Model Dwellings on the corner of Wentworth Street and Goulston Street. The same block of flats where, less than two months earlier, the legend, 'The Juwes are the men that will not be blamed for nothing' was scribbled in white chalk on the stairwell above a dirty, bloodstained piece of apron. Where had this bit of cloth come from and what had happened to provoke this rough graffiti? The blood-soaked piece of cloth was proved beyond any doubt to belong to Catherine Eddowes, who just an hour before it was discovered had been the fourth victim of Britain's most notorious serial killer. Apart from anything else, it was proof that Jack the Ripper knew Wentworth Dwellings well. Had my Aunt Carrie really met the man who had carried out this horrible and shocking deed? And was she lucky to have escaped with her life? Everything that happened in this part of London at the time was overshadowed by the spectral phantom popularly known as Jack the Ripper but somehow our family always felt it had a close connection to this 'apparition from Hell'.

And as if that wasn't enough there was one further connection to Jack the Ripper as my great-uncle, Jacob Levy, my grandpa's brother, has been mentioned in some books as a possible Ripper suspect, even the prime suspect by some authors! It was thought that the description of a man seen talking to Catherine Eddowes just before her murder, fitted Jacob perfectly and, given his previous history and his intimate knowledge of Wentworth Dwellings, there seemed every likelihood that it could be him. This previous history was that he was sentenced to twelve months' imprisonment back in 1886, but was declared insane and instead sent to the Essex County Asylum. He was later released, but in 1890 was again committed to an asylum, this time the Asylum for General Paralysis of the Insane at Stone in Kent. Observations during his term there included testimony from his wife, who complained that he almost ruined their butcher's business: 'He also feels,' she added, 'that if he is not restrained he will do some violence to someone; he complains about hearing strange noises; cries for no reason; feels compelled to do acts that his conscience cannot stand; and has a conscience of a feeling of exaltation.' His wife also revealed that he had formerly been a shrewd businessman and that 'he does not sleep at nights and wanders around aimlessly for hours'.

At 7.52 p.m. on the evening of the 29 July 1891 Jacob finally died at the asylum from 'Paralysis brought on by the serious sexually transmitted disease syphilis', indicating the possibility of liaisons with the Aldgate/Whitechapel prostitutes.

Nothing was ever proved of course, but our family was certainly interwoven closely with the whole Jack the Ripper saga.

Mum grew up in the Dwellings with an ever-expanding number of siblings – there were still two more to come – until, when she was twelve, she lost her father, my grandfather, to bronchitis, pulmonary tuberculosis and exhaustion – at least that's what the death certificate said. Shortly after this, at the age of just thirteen, she left school and went to work in Toff Levy's cigar factory. Like many other cigar and cigarette firms of that time it was situated in the Aldgate area. The work itself was all done by hand and was therefore very labour intensive and teenage girls were a cheap source for this labour.

The work involved was not physically demanding but it did take skill and experience to do it properly. Mum was one of dozens of girls all sitting at benches along the length of the factory floor. The tobacco was delivered to the benches in boxes and sorted into two types, shredded to use for the filling and whole leaves to be used as the wrapping. A specially designed knife was used to cut the leaf to shape and then this would be filled with the shredded tobacco, not too much, not too little, and rolled to make the cigar. Experienced cigar makers, as Mum became, could produce hundreds and hundreds of identical cigars every day.

As she grew through her teens and into her early twenties, Mum turned into a graceful, good-looking young woman with jet-black hair, deep brown eyes and of medium height and slender build. Unlike the stereotype, which it was always our fate to suffer, she did not have a particularly large nose nor did she have a very swarthy complexion, having instead a rather delicate skin tone, probably owing to the fact that her ancestors had lived in this country for something like two hundred years. When out in the street, there is no doubt that she turned the heads of many boys as she made her way to and from work.

A few days after her twenty-first birthday she was promoted at work and put in charge of about half a dozen other girls. There was no extra pay for this increased responsibility but she didn't mind as, although her basic job was still rolling cigars, she did have to take some time off this intensive and repetitive work to help the others and deal with any problems that might arise. One of the girls she was told to look after was a new girl and it was Mum's job to teach her the ropes. This new girl's name was Sarah Jacobs. As they got to know each other better they began to get on very well at work and, when they got the chance, they would laugh and joke together, with their main topic of conversation being boys. They even went out a few times in the evening after work. One day as they were leaving the factory, Mum casually asked Sarah who that handsome young man was that sometimes met her at the gate.

Sarah spluttered. 'Handsome!' she choked. 'That's my brother Jack. Don't tell him he's handsome, his head is big enough as it is.'

Mum's eyes lit up as she pulled a cigarette packet out of her pocket, took one and offered them to Sarah. 'Your brother? How about you should introduce us then?'

Sarah smiled. 'So suddenly I'm a *shadkhen* already?'

Mum blushed, 'Don't talk such *narrishkeit*. I'm not interested in that way.'

'Then why you should want an introduction, Becky?'

Mum smiled and shook her head as if to say this conversation is over.

Two days later, Jack was at the gate to meet Sarah. Mum took her opportunity and skipped over to speak to him. 'Jack,' she said before her friend could say anything, 'how nice to meet you. Sarah has told me so much about you.'

And those were the first words spoken between the two people destined to become my parents. Jack, or John as he was known formally, was actually a couple of years younger than Mum and was born in Bell Lane, just a stone's throw from the Dwellings. He had gone to the Jews' Free School also in Bell Lane, and, like everyone else in his class, left school at the age of thirteen. As the East End was the centre of the furniture trade at the time many boys found themselves going on to work in one capacity or the other in it. In consultation with his father, my grandfather David, Dad chose to be apprenticed to a French-polisher.

Mum and Dad got married on St Valentine's Day, 1914, and moved into my Aunt Betsy's house, renting a couple of rooms from Mum's sister. Just over two months later, on 30 April, their first child, my sister Julie, was born.

When war broke out, on 4 August that year, Dad had no desire to join up before he was made to. But, although he preferred not to rush into war, he did decide to do his bit in another way, as, on 21 December 1915, the shortest and darkest day of the year, when the lamps all over Europe were well and truly out, I was born. Dad used to joke afterwards that I was his real contribution to the war effort.

Eventually, in 1916, he received his call-up papers and he went along for his medical at the Poplar Army Recruitment Office, where he was found to be suffering from flat feet and unsuitable for front-line duties. Because of this, although he was recruited into the army, he was never sent to the trenches and spent the war on the home front, being placed in the Military Police. A lucky escape, many would say. He was assigned to the London Docks, quite close to his home, where his job mostly consisted of patrolling the area and looking out for anyone stealing from the goods landed on the dockside and watching out for deserters who might have stowed away trying to get home. Considering he was exempted from the front line because he had flat feet, it always seemed a bit curious to me that his wartime job entailed spending most of the day walking!

Although working close to home, he was not allowed to live at home, being stationed in nearby barracks instead. Because he wasn't around to protect his family, he thought it best if Mum, Julie and I went to stay with his parents in Gateshead Place in Mile End for the duration. It was here, early in 1918, that my brother Davy was born. As you can see, being in barracks didn't stop Dad getting home on the odd occasion.

In 1918, Dad's flat feet became even more of an issue and he was invalided out of the army altogether. Perhaps it was all that walking round the docks that had exacerbated his condition. Once discharged, he gathered up his little family and set off for pastures new to a house in Palmer Street.

CHAPTER TWO

THE TENTERGROUND AND PULLOCKS, 1915–26

'Come 'ere, you little schmuck!' I was in trouble with Mr Lipschitz yet again. And all because I shouted out, ''Evening, Mr Lipshit,' as I ran past him on the stairs. Was it my fault I kept forgetting the 'z' at the end of his name? 'You show a bit of respect and call me by my proper name or I'll speak to your mother,' he shouted after me as I ran out in to the street. His threat didn't worry me as Mum had no time for him anyway. The first time he told her what I'd said, she took me to one side and said, 'Don't you worry about old Shitty Lips, he's just a bloody Pullock. He's got no right to be here anyway.'

Jack Lipschitz was a tailor who lived on the ground floor of our three-storey house in Palmer Street. He was a recent immigrant, hence to us a Pullock.

Palmer Street was in Spitalfields, in an area known as the

Tenterground, a name which referred to the fact that this had once been a large open area used for drying newly manufactured cloth. While still wet, this cloth was hooked onto frames called tenters and stretched taut so that the cloth would dry flat and square. The area the tenters stood on was known as a tenterground. There were several around but this particular one in Spitalfields was first established in the seventeenth century by refugee French Huguenot weavers, who were fleeing religious persecution. The establishment of their clothing industry in the area gave rise to a number of the local street names, so, as well as Tenter Street itself, there were names such as Fashion Street and Petticoat Lane.

By the early nineteenth century, the Huguenot weavers had left the area, and between 1829 and 1850, the Tenterground was developed for housing being populated mainly by Dutch Jews, who had immigrated from the Netherlands, which gave rise to the area being generally known in the early days as the Dutch Tenterground.

By the time we moved there, well over 90 per cent of the population was Jewish. But just because we were all Jewish didn't mean we all got on. There was a big divide between those Dutch Jewish families who had been in England a long time and now saw themselves as basically English Jews and those who arrived in the late nineteenth or early twentieth century as a result of the latest pogrom in some Eastern European state or other, mainly following the assassination of the Russian Tsar Alexander II by a Jew, in 1881.

All foreign Jews were called 'Pullocks' by English Jews, no matter which part of Europe they came from. Pullock was a slang word for Polish. Should Mum be having a few words with a Pullock she would tell her to go back to Russia, geography not being her strong point. Then again, if we had words with a gentile family they would tell us to go back to Palestine, so it evened itself out.

Unlike these Pullocks, our family could trace its roots in England back to the 1660s and we were amongst the first Jewish families to be allowed into England after Oliver Cromwell had revoked the old medieval prohibition, the 1290 Edict of Expulsion, on Jews living in the country. Having been anglicised for so long we spoke no Hebrew, though our talk did contain a fair smattering of Yiddish, due to mixing with so many other Jews in everyday life where Yiddish was almost a first language for some.

The Tenterground consisted of six streets in the form of a ladder, the two uprights being Shepherd Street and Tenter Street, and going across like four rungs were, starting at the Commercial Street end, Butler Street, Freeman Street, Palmer Street and Tilley Street. This complex was encompassed by White's Row, Bell Lane, Wentworth Street and finally Commercial Street.

There were about ten houses on each side of our street. They were terraced with three floors, ground, first and top. Each floor had two rooms, the front room overlooking the street and the back room overlooking the yard. All the downstairs front windows had shutters.

When anybody called at the house and the front door was shut the recognised procedure was one knock for the ground floor, two for the first floor and of course three for the second floor. Most times though, the doors were just left open and if anyone wanted to come and see us they'd just walk in and up to our flat. Mum and her friends in particular were forever going in and out of each other's houses either to borrow something or just for a natter. No worries about anyone breaking in to steal anything as we never had anything worth stealing.

The house we lived in was home to three families, each occupying one floor. Mr Lipschitz and his family lived on the ground floor. He was a working tailor who used his two rooms as a workshop.

He had a sewing machine in his front room where his wife and their daughter Hetty worked. There was also a sewing machine and long bench for ironing in the back. He did all the ironing whilst his brother, Lippy, worked the back room sewing machine. All the work was stored in a big shed behind the house. In the summer Jack Lipschitz did all the pressing in the yard, where there was a brick fire for the irons. These four people lived and slept there too; how they found the room, I never knew.

Up one flight of stairs to a small landing saw the door to Solly Norton's two rooms, which he shared with his wife Polly and son Ascher, who was about my age. Although they lived in the same slum building as us and with as much room as us, they seemed to be a bit better off, probably because there were only three mouths to feed. They had a proper matching table and chairs as well as a proper sideboard. There was also a big pink upholstered armchair, which looked very inviting but seemed to be permanently occupied by Solly.

More importantly, they also had the first gramophone I ever

saw, the type with the big horn. When I was older I would often go down and play with Ascher, just so I could hear this marvel of modern technology. The records they played most were of the old music hall stars like Marie Lloyd, Gus Elen and Florrie Forde. The songs were all very familiar to me because my mum and dad were great lovers of the old music hall and were always singing their songs round the house; Dad in particular used to give us full renditions of many a Gus Elen song at the drop of a hat. Ascher also had a few 'up-to-date' jazz records with artistes such as Louis Armstrong, Paul Whiteman and Jelly Roll Morton, though I don't think his parents were too keen on them – a bit too modern – so we only played them when they were out.

The Nortons kept a fruit stall in that world-famous market, Petticoat Lane, or, as it was known to us, simply the Lane. To residents of the Tenterground, the Lane was the part of Wentworth Street that ran between Commercial Street and Middlesex Street rather than Middlesex Street itself.

Up another flight to another very small landing where the door to our front room faced you. The landing then continued as a narrow passage to the right, showing the back-room door.

When we first moved in there were only the five of us, but this gradually increased to ten as more and more brothers and sisters came along over the years. Living on the top floor with this ever-expanding family brought with it many problems, particularly for Mum, not the least of which was getting the ever-present perambulator up and down the stairs, accompanied by at least one or two toddlers who would occasionally take it upon themselves to tumble down the stairs.

The fact that we only had one lavatory between the three families and that it was outside in the back yard along with the one (cold) water tap didn't help either, as we had to carry up all the water we required and then take the dirty water down again to dispose of it. There was no inside loo or water.

CHAPTER THREE

HUMPTY LOGIE, DOLL-DOLL AND JULIE BOTTLES, 1919–26

'What the bloody 'ell's happened to you?' Mum took one look at the blood pouring from my nose and demanded an explanation.

'It's Ruby Kutner,' I replied. 'He did it.'

'I expect you deserved it then.'

'I didn't do anyfing,' I protested. 'I was playin' with Davy [my younger brother] out in the street when he came along swingin' an old tin can round on a piece of string and 'it me on the nose.'

'Right! Come with me, we'll see about this.' And even though she was heavily pregnant with yet another prospective baby Jacobs, she dragged me back out into the street to find the aforesaid Ruby Kutner. She didn't have to go far as he was still outside swinging his tin can around.

'Oi, Kutner!' Mum shouted. 'Stop swinging that bloody can round already. It's dangerous. Look what you've done to mein Ikey.'

'Piss off, you stupid *yente*, I'll do what I like. You don't own the street.'

'Don't you talk to me like that,' Mum replied. 'Wait till I tell Ikey's father.'

'Oh, I'm so scared,' Ruby laughed.

That night, when Dad came home, Mum gave him a full account of what had occurred. Now if Ruby had been my age he would have told me to hit him back, that was one of the rules we lived by in those days, but as he was a couple of years older and had been saucy to Mum, Dad thought he would go across the road and have a word with master Reuben. When he got no answer to his persistent knocking on the door he just kicked the front panel in leaving a gaping hole in the middle of the door. Feeling that justice had been done he left it at that. The Kutners nailed a board across the gap and that's how it stayed until the day we moved away years later.

Ruby Kutner was well-known as a local tearaway and was often involved in fisticuffs with another young resident of the street, Alfie Ruffel. I well remember the day they squared up in the middle of Palmer Street and battled all the way round to the top of Freeman Street via Shepherd Street.

There were many other characters in our street. In fact there were four other Jacobs families living in Palmer Street. Two of them were Dad's uncles. The first was Uncle Harry, who lived a few doors down from us with his wife Fanny and their four children. We never had much to do with them. Mum called

Fanny 'Humpty Logie', probably because she had a bit of a hunchback, and said she was 'stuck up'. Uncle Freddy lived opposite them. Although he was Dad's uncle, he was actually five years younger than him, the youngest of a long line of aunts and uncles. He lived with his wife, called Doll-Doll by Mum.

The other two Jacobs families were not relations. One, Tingle Jacobs, owned some low loaders which were parked in the street and he would be loading and unloading cargo all day. The father of the fourth Jacobs family was known as 'Fat' Jacobs. His soubriquet fitted him to a tee; he was small and very rotund. He spoke in a quiet voice with a pronounced German accent. He had two sons; the elder, Maxi, became a good pal of mine.

Our house was second on the right going from Shepherd Street. In the first house lived Joe Wallenstein, a toy merchant. Between his shop and our house was a wall along which he often lined up lots of boxes of dolls. When I was about six years old, my cousin, Ikey Isaacs, then in his early twenties, was up our house. He took me to one side and said, 'Ikey, can you go down and get me a doll? Make sure nobody's looking when you take it.' Not knowing any better, I did what I was told by the grown-up. I found out later that Ikey was a bit of a *gonif* and spent several spells in prison.

Next to us on the other side lived Esther and Marky Woolf with their five boys, just like the well-known Fry's chocolate bar of the time! One of them, Manny Woolf, was a particular friend of mine. The youngest son Mickey did a bit of professional boxing when he grew up, calling himself Mickey Woods. He never got very far.

Fourth house down saw Fanny Robalus, a widow with her daughter, Mary. Then Mrs Sarlavy, and her niece Ray Ray Papier. Mrs Sarlavy was a nice old dear. We called her 'old mother rinking hat' because she always wore a dark woollen hat.

On to Dickie and Hester Saunders. They were very friendly with Mum and Dad. They had two children, Morrie and Rosie. I was very good friends with Morrie and stayed in touch with him long after we left the Tenterground.

Then came Joey Waterman; I can't remember if he had any parents. He was about fifteen or sixteen years old. He was a milkman and always seemed to carry a wet cloth about with him. Whenever he saw me he would try to whack me with it.

Ray Ruffel, a widow (I wonder now if she was a war widow) with two children, Alfie and Doris, came next.

Finally, on our side of the street, came Bottles. He was always addressed thus, never heard him called anything else, with his wife, Julie Bottles, and their two children.

Across the street at our end lived Sarah Rosenberg with her husband Judah, and son Woolfy.

One morning when I was very young, probably about four or five, I was outside with Mum when Sarah came rushing out of her house screaming, 'Help me! Help me! Somebody help me! Judah's trying to kill me!' Although there were a number of people out in the street astonishingly to my young mind no one took any notice of her or went to see what was wrong and just let her carry on shouting and screaming while they continued doing whatever it was they were doing. Sarah meanwhile was getting more and more hysterical and eventually I couldn't stand

20

it any more. So, I finally yelled, 'Mum, Mum, that woman says someone is trying to kill her, shouldn't we do something?'

Mum barely looked up from scrubbing the front door step. 'Don't take no notice, Ikey, she's forever doing that. She just likes the attention.'

Although I was still a bit concerned I felt that if Mum said not to worry then I wouldn't. Eventually Sarah calmed down and just sauntered back indoors to face her husband.

Over the years I lived there, I came to realise that Mum was right as this little scenario was played out every few months. Mind you, the more I got to know Judah, the more I thought he might really be hurting Sarah as he was a funny sort of bloke and frankly I wouldn't have put anything past him. But no one else ever seemed to care and I never actually saw her with any bruises. Their son Woolfy was a nice sort, always smiling. I got on all right with him and he never seemed worried about his parents so I guess Mum was right.

Of course wife beating was not unknown and was probably far more common than it is today, but amongst our mainly Jewish community I didn't know of any cases where this happened.

The Kutner household, which I have already mentioned, was directly opposite us. Living with Ruby and his family was his grandfather, Myer Kutner, an itinerant glazier who used to walk the streets with a frame on his back containing sheets of glass.

Going on past the Kutners was Mottle Simons with his wife and two daughters. He once cycled all the way to Brighton unbeknown to his wife to look for work. It must have been quite a while before he returned, sadly, still jobless.

Natie Shine was the third house from the end; a very staunch Labour man. I believe he must have been some sort of agent for that illustrious party because he always turned his front room into a Labour stronghold at election time. During the 1924 general election he stuck a poster in his window urging us to vote for Harry Gosling, whose kindly face looked out upon us from the poster. His opponent in this parliamentary battle was one Major Kiley, a Liberal. As we local youth came almost exclusively from Labour families we took to the street with our battle hymn:

> 'Vote, vote, vote for Harry Gosling
> Knock old Kiley in the eye
> Cos Kiley is a *yok* and he's got a pointed cock
> And we won't vote for Kiley any more.'

The penultimate family were the Strongs, Harry, his wife and two sons. Joey Strong was about my age, the other son was younger. Harry dealt in china. Every Sunday morning he would be down the Lane auctioning dinner services, tea sets and other items of chinaware.

The method he employed was to spread the sets he was selling out on a big metal tray and clap his hands above his head a few times to attract a crowd. Once there were enough gathered round, he'd begin by bouncing the dinner service up and down on the tray and barking:

'Look at this dinner service! You'll never see another like it. It's unique. The only one ever made with this pattern. Genuine Wedgwood. It's worth a fortune, but, ladies and gentlemen, you're in luck today as I'm in a particularly good mood cos my gee-gees came in yesterday so I've decided to share my good luck with you and give it away for practically nothing. So, I'm not asking £1, not even 10 bob, 5 bob, half a crown. It's yours for 2 bob!' At which point he would strike the tray hard with the flat of his hand. 'Who'll be the first to put their silver down?' All the while he was doing this he kept on bouncing the pieces up and down till finally he stopped with the final line, 'All right! You're robbing me blind but it's yours for just two tanners.' Several hands would go up and he'd point to one, saying, 'My kids'll starve tonight but you should worry at least you got a bargain!'

With that, he'd give one final bounce of the dinner set, gather it up and the proud buyer would hand over his shilling and take it away.

As soon as the purchaser had gone, he would reach under his stall and take out another dinner service, identical to the 'unique' Wedgwood set he'd just sold, and the process would be repeated.

He used to fascinate me and I'd go down the Lane sometimes just to watch his performance; in all the times I saw him do this, he never once dropped or broke a single piece of crockery.

Finally there was Nobby Josephs with his mum and dad. They were greengrocers and also had a stall in the Lane. Nobby had bright red hair; he was a few years my senior.

CHAPTER FOUR

LOKSHEN SOUP, JAM JARS AND KEATING'S POWDER, 1919–26

'Sorry, Becky, but we'll have to tighten our belts next week. My job's come to an end. There's no work next week and I really can't see when I'll be able to get some more.' I'm not sure exactly how old I was when I first heard those words as Dad walked through the door on his return from work, though it obviously wasn't the first time he'd said it and I didn't really know what it meant, but I knew it couldn't be good as Mum started sobbing and said, 'Oh, Jack, we can't keep going on like this.' As I grew older this was to become a fairly regular occurrence as Dad would often return home from work on a Friday afternoon, announcing that we would all have to 'tighten our belts' as he had no work to go to the following week. Somehow, though, she, and we, always did carry on.

On this particular night, however, Mum reminded Dad that

we had company that night. 'Oh no,' she wept, 'Woolfy and Betsy are supposed to be coming round tonight. What can we do?' Dad shrugged. 'We've got this week's money,' he said. 'We can worry about next week next week.'

Woolfy was my uncle and Dad's younger brother. Betsy, of course, was his wife and my aunt. They used to come round about once a month on a Friday evening to eat with us. Friday was the main meal of the week for Jewish families as it heralded in Shabbos. The meal when Uncle Woolfy came round was always the same – chicken and *lokshen* soup, accompanied by baked potatoes and rice. The soup was made by boiling up a whole chicken in a pot of water with carrots, parsnips and celery, a pinch of saffron and a large helping of *lokshen* (known to non-Jewish families as vermicelli). When the soup was ready, the chicken was taken out, jointed and carved and served up on a plate with the baked potatoes and rice while the soup was served up in a bowl.

This particular night when Uncle Woolfy and Aunt Betsy turned up, Mum and Dad acted as if nothing was wrong. As usual, Mum was baking the potatoes and rice in one large dish in our small coal-fired range oven, the rice on the bottom with the spuds on top and round the sides, while the soup was merrily boiling away on the open-ring gas stove next to it.

'Ikey, get the plates down, will you,' Mum commanded. I got down what passed for our best china, though it was somewhat old and battered with many chips and cracks and consisted of plates and bowls of different patterns, the most common of which was the Willow Pattern, a highly successful English design based on traditional Chinese images. The

Victorians even invented a plausible-sounding 'traditional Chinese' tale to accompany it, the pattern supposed to depict the tragic story of the forbidden love between a Mandarin's daughter and the Mandarin's accountant, a man too far below his daughter's status to be allowed to marry her. In some versions though, it all ends happily as the two lovers turn into doves and fly off together. Mum used to tell me the story often, but in her usual manner, she managed to get the whole thing completely mixed up and the two lovers turned into two children from Dover rather than doves. Still, as long as they made their escape and lived happily ever after, who cares who or what they turned into!

Over dinner, Uncle Woolfy said he had an announcement to make. This sounded interesting, I thought. But all he said was 'Betsy's expecting.' This didn't make much sense to me as he didn't explain what Betsy was expecting, but Mum and Dad seemed to think it was great news. Mum got up and threw her arms round Betsy, hugging her so tight that Betsy almost had to push her off. Dad said, 'About time too, Woolfy. I was beginning to think you didn't know what it was for. What is it, seven years you been married now?' Betsy blushed but Woolfy just laughed. This all seemed very mysterious to me but if Mum and Dad were happy, it was all right with me.

'This calls for a celebration,' Mum said. 'Get the cola and some cups, Ikey.' I'm sure she would have preferred to celebrate with a glass of wine, but even in good times that was far more than we could afford. So I went to our food cupboard, which was actually an orange box with two compartments covered by a curtain nailed high up on the wall to the right of the front door.

There I took out a bottle of cola, which we used to buy from a travelling merchant called N. Laid, and put it on the table, then I went to the dresser and took out a couple of cracked cups, one without a handle, for our guests while the rest of us had to settle for some stone jam jars, which passed for cups in our house. Dad opened the bottle, known as a Codd bottle, which had a glass marble in the top that had to be pushed down into a recess just below the neck, the recess being just narrow enough to stop it falling into the bottle, and poured out the cola. Salutations of 'long life' and '*mazel tov*' rang out around the table. I was still a bit mystified by what this was all about, but the cola was a welcome change from the normal cup of water.

After dinner was over, Mum said she had a favour to ask of Uncle Woolfy. 'Have you any work going for Jack?' she asked, getting straight to the point. Dad was a French-polisher by trade and Woolfy was a cabinet maker, so sometimes he was able to put a bit of work Dad's way. But this time, Uncle Woolfy sadly shook his head and said, 'Things are bad all round in the furniture trade at the moment, Becky. I have very little work on myself. I'm sorry, Jack.' This short conversation seemed to bring the grown-ups down to earth after their happiness at Betsy's news and a more sombre mood settled over everyone until it was time for Uncle Woolfy and Aunt Betsy to leave.

I must have been about seven when we heard the news that Aunt Betsy was expecting. By this time there were eight of us, as Mum had been producing new babies at regular intervals. I was followed by Davy, then Woolfy (known to us all as Bill), Abie and, just a couple months ago, the latest arrival, Joey. As it happened, Mum must also have been pregnant just like Aunt

Betsy, although probably too early to know, as yet another small Jacobs joined the world a short while after Aunt Betsy's baby. This was Manny, who was the last to be born in Palmer Street.

Even without Manny, bedtime was a bit of a challenge as it always was. First of all, when Mum said, 'Time for bed' she made us all line up and took us out to the back yard so we could do a wee before going to bed. Back upstairs, Julie took over and marched us boys into the back room where there were two single beds. As soon as we were inside and free of parents, we started playing up, nothing too bad, but we would stick our tongues out at Julie and generally make things as difficult as possible for her as she tried to get us into bed.

Our favourite game was to get into a long oblong box that stood about 18 inches high from the floor against the left hand wall. Formally, it was a coal box where we stored our coal for the coal hearth which housed the range and oven, but to us it was a bus, a train, a police car or anything else we wanted it to be.

On this particular night it was a fire engine. 'Ding-a-ling, ding-a-ling,' Davy squawked as he jumped in the front and turned the imaginary steering wheel. 'Fireman Bill, man the ladder,' I commanded. With Abie joining in as well, even though he was only two, Julie could see she had her hands full. 'Stop it,' she shouted, 'get to bed or I'll tell Dad.'

As it happens, she didn't have to carry out her threat as Mum threw the door open and said, 'What's going on here? Why aren't you all in bed? Julie, get them to bed already!' Although her intervention made us get out of the coal box and get ready for bed, the real reason for her visit was to bring in the night-time pail, which she placed in the corner of the room. This was to save us having to go downstairs and out into the yard in the middle of the night if we felt the urge to go to the loo.

In fact, going to bed was quite a simple procedure as we had no pyjamas to change into. At that age I had never even heard of such things. It was just jersey, trousers, boots and socks off and into bed in our shirts. Julie slept in one bed with Abie, while we three older boys slept like sardines, heads top and bottom, all legs meeting in the middle. Baby Joey slept with Mum and Dad in their bed in the living room.

The following morning after we'd all trooped down to the yard for the toilet and a cold water wash under the tap, we came back upstairs for breakfast. This consisted of a slice of bread and marge each. As we were eating, Mum started sobbing again. Dad got up and put his arm round her, 'Don't cry, Becky, we've been here before, remember. We'll manage.'

'Why can't you get yourself a proper job?' she said bitterly.

'I do have a proper job,' Dad replied, 'there's just not much work around at the moment. We're not the only family suffering. On Monday, I'll have a look round to see if there's anyone needs some lino laying.'

As well as being a French-polisher, Dad was also a very good lino-layer and as he knew quite a few furniture shops along the Whitechapel and Mile End Roads he would get the occasional job doing that.

'If not I'll go down the club and see if there's any work going there until I can find some more French-polishing work.'

From time to time he would work as a waiter at the Netherlands Club in Bell Lane. When I was a bit older I used to boast to my school friends that my father was the head waiter at the Bell Lane Club, which is what we called it. He wasn't of course, and waiting was really only a stop gap until he could find some proper work.

'That's all very well, Jack,' said Mum, 'but we're still going to have to tighten our belts in the meantime.'

'Well, we've still got some money from last week's work,' Dad reminded her, 'so let's at least have a good weekend and then worry about what we're going to do later.'

So, on that Saturday we ate quite well. For lunch we had more bread and marge, while Joey had some semolina washed down with some milk from his bottle which was just an ordinary medicine bottle with a teat.

In the evening we had our main meal of the day, dinner, which on this day consisted of fried ox heart with rice boiled with shredded cabbage and currants and boiled potatoes garnished with a knob of marge. Sometimes, on other good days, we might have lamb's liver or sausages instead of the ox heart.

Sunday saw us blow nearly all the rest of the money we had with a salt beef dinner, which was really my favourite. Cooked with carrots, cabbage and potatoes in the same saucepan, I enjoyed the fat most of all, even though it always gave me a bilious headache. It was so good that I ate it anyway even knowing what the consequences would be.

Work or no work, money or no money, Sunday night was bath night. As the two eldest, Julie and I, were called on to help out in this procedure. 'Ikey, get the bath out and Julie, start bringing up the water,' Mum ordered. So off I went to the back room, to take the tin bath off the nail that Dad had banged into the wall to hang it on and brought it in to the front room and placed it on the floor in the living room. Julie meanwhile had started the slow and laborious process of going down to the backyard with our kettle, filling it up with water and bringing it back up the two flights of stairs to pour into a bowl on the gas stove. After I'd brought the bath in, I helped Julie by getting an old cracked enamel jug we kept in the cupboard and running up and down the stairs with her till the bowl was filled. Once Mum felt the water was warm enough she'd pour the bowl into the bath. We had to fill the bowl several times to make a bathful. By the time the last bowl was poured in, I expect the first lot of water Mum had tipped in had gone cold, but there just wasn't any other way of filling the bath.

Julie, as the oldest and the only girl, was always the first to get in the bath, then the rest of us went in in pairs. Once in the bath, Mum would give us all a good scrubbing with a bar of Lifebuoy soap. She'd then pay special attention to our hair and used some soft soap to destroy any head lice and nits we might have, thus keeping the notorious 'Nitty Nora' (as schools' nit nurses were called) at a distance. In appearance this soap looked like thick grease. It was bought in the oil shop and sold by weight and wrapped in newspaper.

Head lice were also kept at bay with regular haircuts. Dad always did these himself. He'd give us all a short back and sides with the clippers he had and shave our necks with a cut-throat razor.

As well as destroying the bugs and lice on our bodies, Mum would spend an inordinate amount of time in her perpetual battle on fleas, bugs and lice in our flat. Keating's Powder was her favourite weapon in this war as it boasted it killed all lice and bedbugs. She religiously applied it to all bed springs and mattresses at least twice a week, but it always seemed to me that the bugs were unaware of Keating's boast as they just carried on minding their own business and multiplying at an alarming rate. Every now and then, in an attempt to thin out these unwanted hordes, Dad would employ a sulphur candle, which gave off acrid fumes when you applied a match to it. Windows and doors had to be sealed to prevent any leakage. Alas, after each fumigation they never stayed thinned out for long. They must have thought they had squatters' rights.

This fight against germs, lice and bugs went on incessantly. Carbolic was yet another aid in keeping the germs at bay. Bought as a liquid it was added to a pail of water and Mum would set to scrubbing the floors, which were mainly bare boards. Sunlight Soap, scrubbing brush and flannel were the other articles required in this operation.

CHAPTER FIVE

STALE BREAD, CRACKED EGGS AND THE BUN HOUSE, 1919–26

With practically all of Dad's money gone, Mum had to think of how to eke out the little we had left until Dad could find some more work. So, very early on Monday morning, while Dad made his rounds of the furniture shops in Whitechapel looking for work as a lino-layer, Mum turned to Julie and me and said, 'You two'll have to skip school this morning and go out and find what food you can for as little as you can. Ikey, you go off to Funnel's and get some stale bread,' and gave me sixpence. As I opened the door, Mum called after me, 'Don't forget the pillowcase, Ikey!' I raced down the stairs and went off to our local baker's with my pillowcase. You had to go very early in the morning as many other families were in the same plight as us and were having to do the same thing. We were not always lucky but, on this day when I asked for 'sixpenn'orth of stale bread, please' I was very lucky as the lady in the shop threw five loaves of differing shapes and sizes in various stages of staleness into my pillow case. When I got them home, Mum broke out into a big smile and patted me on the head, saying, 'Well done, Ikey! That'll keep us going for a bit. Let's sort them out.' We then sorted out the fresher, or should I say the least stale, for eating, and the remainder were put aside to be soaked down for a bread pudding. Delicious.

Julie meanwhile had been dispatched to Kramer's, a big provision store in the Lane, on the corner of Wentworth Street and Goulston Street, to get some eggs. The eggs were sold outside the shop from a long stall on which were placed four or five long wooden crates of eggs. The lady who sold the eggs stood with her back to the wall behind the stall. Julie was also given sixpence, but she had a basin rather than a pillowcase. When she reached the stall, she said to the lady, 'Sixpenn'orth of cracks, please.' The lady then put in a dozen cracked eggs from a tray marked, 'best new laid'. Whether they were new laid or not was very debatable. As always, when Julie got them home and Mum cracked them open, at least three or four of them were found to have gone bad.

Mum gave me and Julie a bit of crust each as a reward and then said, 'Time to get some washing done.' This was a regular Monday-morning chore, whether Dad was in work or out of it. Once again I had to get the bath out, only for washing this time. I placed it on our table rather than the floor, and Julie and I had to bring the water up from the yard. A similar process to bath night took place as Mum heated up the water and poured it into the bath. Regular washing of clothes was, of course, along with the never-ending battle against the invasion of lice and bugs, all part of trying to keep our family clean.

Once Mum had decided the bath had enough water in, she put all the clothes in and scattered some Rinso or Hudson's Washing Powder over them and left them for a few minutes to soak, while she placed our washboard next to the bath. Then she would take the clothes out one by one, place them on the washboard and give them a good hard vigorous rub with some Sunlight Soap. It was bloody hard work and, of course, while she was sweating away doing this, she had to keep an eye on all us children, which in itself was a full-time job. Most times, she would just tell us to go out and play in the street. It seems funny to say that in this day and age, but off we'd go, including the two-year-old Abie, in fact all of us except the baby, to play outside. Normally she would place Joey in his large makeshift cot, made from yet another orange box. Although we were very young to be outside on our own, there was not much fear of traffic in those days, though I do remember that one day when we were jumping on and off Tingle Jacobs's low loaders as we often did – the idea being that as many boys as possible would jump on and then one of us would shout out 'whip behind Guv'nor' when we saw Mr Jacobs or one of his men approaching and we would all jump off – I gave a big leap off the back and got run over by a horse-drawn cart that was coming along. Luckily I was unhurt.

That evening, Dad got back quite late. He sat down and took his boots off before saying a word. Then he just shook his head, looked at Mum and said, 'Nothing! No one wants any polishing, no one wants any lino laid and even the bloody club said they've got enough waiters at the moment. It's desperate out there, Becky. Everyone looking for work that doesn't exist. So much for Lloyd George's land fit for sodding heroes.'

Mum started sobbing again. 'What are we going to do, Jack? Ikey got us some stale bread this morning and Julie got some cracked eggs but that was nearly all the money we had.'

'I'll try again tomorrow, but if there's nothing then, we might have to call in the Relieving Officer.' This was the first time I can remember Dad looking so unhappy and almost defeated. In my eyes, he had always been such a strong, happy man. Things must be bad, I thought.

Mum started crying even harder. 'No, Jack, supposing they put us in the Workhouse. Can't we try the Board of Guardians first?' The Workhouse was a threat that hung over all poor families at the time. It was the most hated institution in the country and families did all they could to avoid being incarcerated behind its dark forbidding walls. It wasn't prison of course, but it might just as well have been. Families were split up and the men and boys put to work on hard labour, while the women too had to 'earn their keep' while trying to look after any young children they had. It was to be avoided at all costs. But if you had no money and couldn't feed yourself or pay the rent, sometimes there was just no alternative other than begging on the streets.

'They won't put us in the Workhouse, Becky,' Dad said. 'I'll make sure of that! But perhaps you could try the Guardians tomorrow to see if they can help.'

The following day, Mum took us brood of kids along to

the Jewish Board of Guardians' office in Middlesex Street where we joined a long queue of people waiting to be seen. Eventually it was our turn and the man behind the desk said, 'Hello, Mrs Jacobs, haven't seen you for a while. How bad is it this time?'

Mum replied that Jack was out of work and had been trying to get another job but so far had been unsuccessful, 'I'm sure it won't be for long. He'll be back in work in no time, but if you could give us something to tide us over we would be very grateful.'

The man drummed his fingers on the table. 'You know, Mrs Jacobs,' he said eventually, 'it wouldn't hurt if maybe you came to *shul* more often. We like to help Jews down on their luck, but we have to be careful how much charity we give out, and maybe the more deserving get the most.'

Mum started crying. 'Can't you see the handful I've got here with all my *kinder*? We just don't have time for shul. But I promise we'll come as often as we can, believe me.'

The man gave a snort and said, 'Yes, I'm, sure Mrs Jacobs. I'll give you a couple of tickets this morning, but maybe you should take notice of what I said already.'

The tickets he gave us were known as BMC tickets, which stood for bread, meat and coal. Their value was 1s. 6d. and they could be exchanged at any shop displaying the notice 'We take BMC tickets'. The tickets had a proviso printed on them saying the shopkeeper was not allowed to give any change; you either bought the exact amount or paid the extra if it was over. The reason for this being that some people might buy a small amount then booze or bet with the change. The shops that displayed the signs were mostly run by Jewish owners and it was to these that we went after obtaining our tickets.

Although they were called bread, meat and coal tickets, they were accepted for any purchases. Mum's priority this morning was to get some veg for a stew, so it was off to Nelly Ragan's in Shepherd Street to get some pot-herbs, carrots, turnips, onions and potatoes as you could get a much greater quantity of these for your 1s. 6d. than meat, and a nice stew would see us through a few days with luck. As there was no actual meat in the stew, Mum also bought an Oxo cube. At that time they were little hard objects which took about an hour to melt but at least they gave you a vague taste of meat.

One other shop we went to when times were hard was Palacci, a small general store in Shepherd Street near White's Row. It was here we would be sent with one of our own cups for a penn'orth of jam or mustard pickles. This was done by weighing the cup first then adding the jam or pickles till a penny's worth was registered. We could also get a penny packet of tea or cocoa here.

We were also fortunate in living near Spitalfields, a big fruit and vegetable market. This was always very busy, especially in the morning when Commercial Street would be choked with moving and parked traffic. All the produce sold there was laid out on sacks, in baskets or in boxes. One of the sights of the market was porters carrying numerous round baskets of produce on their heads. The importance of morning at Spitalfields for us though was that this was the best time to go looking for 'specks'. These were bad oranges or apples thrown into a box which could be scavenged for nothing. Selecting those with half or more salvageable I would take them home where the bad parts were cut away and the remainder eaten. This was also the source of much of our orange box furniture.

As it seemed unlikely the Board of Guardians would be giving us any more tickets in the near future, Mum spent just one of the tickets, saving the other for a few days' time if Dad still hadn't managed to get any work, though in truth, Mum wasn't too concerned that the Board of Guardians had threatened her with no more tickets unless we went to shul once in a while as, fortunately for us, though, I suppose, unfortunately in other ways, there were a number of other smaller charities who dispensed second-hand clothing and BMC tickets, who weren't quite so fussy about who they gave their charity to. Camperdown House in Aldgate was one such place. These places created a band of people known as professional *schnorrers*, who were always to be seen wherever anything was being handed out. They would line up for the clothes and then flog most of what they got, so getting a few bob at a needy person's expense.

As the week wore on, it became obvious that there was just no work around and that we were going to have to continue to rely on charity to see us through. So, in spite of Mum's misgivings, Dad did go and see the Relieving Officer with our famous pillowcase, hoping to get it filled up.

The Relieving Officer was employed by the Ministry of Health to assess claims for support as a result of unemployment or sickness. Although many, like Mum, were afraid this assessment would lead to a spell in the Workhouse, the local Board of Guardians of the Workhouse were in fact more interested in trying to keep families together in their own homes if at all possible as it put less pressure on them to have to house and feed yet more inmates.

When Dad returned from the Bun House, which is what we called the Relieving Officer's establishment, he emptied the pillowcase on to the table and, to our great delight, out fell a large quantity of basic foodstuffs, more stale bread, cracked eggs and the like but the highlight of this haul of food was a stone jar of Hartley's strawberry jam, which I think we finished up in less than an hour! As well as its being a little treat, the empty jar served as another cup for us. An item of foodstuff we weren't so keen on was a piece of very smelly cheese – God knows how old it was! Davy exaggeratedly held his nose and said, 'Phew! That smells like sweaty feet!' Ever afterwards in our house, cheese we obtained from charities was always referred to as sweaty feet.

Dad told us that the Relieving Officer had also given him some money to pay for the rent and gave it to Mum to put away for the next time the rent man called. Looking back on this now, I think we were very lucky to have such a responsible father. I guess many at the time would have just drunk the rent money away, but Dad was a real family man and hardly ever went out for a drink. His first priority was always looking after us.

As winter was approaching, Dad had another idea about where we could get some relief and this was the Soup Kitchen in Butler Street. It opened three nights a week and issued bread, marge, saveloys, sardines and of course soup. The first time Dad went down there, he took me with him. He had to fill in a form – name, address, number in family etc. – which the clerk at the desk stamped and placed on a pile of other such forms.

He then handed over what he called a kettle, though it wasn't like any kettle I'd ever seen. It was a round tin with a lid and metal handle with a thick wire attached to each side, upright when held, lying down the side when not in use. Because of this we always called it our can rather than kettle. These cans had a number stamped on the side depicting how many portions you were to get. Because we had such a large family, ours had the number four stamped on it.

Visiting the Soup Kitchen became a way of life for us over the next few years and it was usually me who Mum and Dad sent along to get our supplies. By opening time, there would usually be a long queue along Butler Street and when the doors opened we would all file in. Once inside, six crash barriers had to be negotiated in a single line till the door leading to the serving area was reached. There would be two men doing the serving, both dressed in white and wearing tall chef's hats. The first one would give me four brick loaves, two packets of Van den Burgh's 'Toma' margarine and two tins of sardines. If you preferred them you could also ask for saveloys here, but then you couldn't get soup as well. It was a case of either/or. I was invariably told to get the soup as we had saveloys once but they were 80 per cent bread so we never got them again.

Having dealt with the grocery department I moved along to the soup giver. He was a great favourite of mine; known by our family as 'the fat cook', he was a stout, domineering man with a fine beard. As I gave him our can he would look me in the eyes and ask '*Fleish* or no *fleish*?' If you did not want any meat you'd say 'No *fleish*'. Now although the meat was, as a rule, 50 per cent fat, I was always instructed to get some, so I would return his gaze and reply in a loud voice, '*Fleish.*' He would then glare at me and go off to a large boiler to get it.

I always took our food home for the family to eat there, but some people had their soup at the kitchen itself. There was a long table with form seating each side, set out between the boilers and the servers, where anybody, Jew or gentile, could go in and sit down to a bowl of soup and a thick slice of bread. They did three different varieties of soup: rice, pea and barley alternately, one variety per night. People who did not want the soup at all but just the groceries were given a metal disc with the portion number stamped on it. Funny, not wanting soup in a soup kitchen.

Every Passover, before they closed for the summer, we would be given four portions of various groceries for the holiday which consisted of four packets of tea and four of coffee, some 'Toma' marge and many other foodstuffs. I loved the smell of the coffee, its aroma came right through the packet, a red packet with Hawkins printed on it. In spite of being to see you through Passover, matzos were not supplied; these were obtainable from the shul. Dad would come back from Duke's Place Shul with about six packets of these crunchy squares. There were two makes, Latimer's, which we disliked as we thought them too hard, and Abrahams and Abrahams', which were a trifle better and the ones Dad normally got.

With a growing family, the other big problem we had when Dad was out of work was finding money for clothes. This particular period of unemployment was to last several weeks and, although there were many cheap second-hand clothing shops and stalls down the Lane, they were still out of our reach financially.

One evening, as we settled down to our dinner of a slice of stale bread and marge, Mum said, 'Jack, we really need to find some way of getting some clothes for the kids. They're all growing up so fast that all their clothes are getting too small.' I was certainly glad to hear this as at the time I was stuck with two pairs of boots I hated and just wanted to get shot of. The first was a pair of girl's high lace-up boots, which I felt highly embarrassed wearing and I had several terrible ribbings at school and amongst my friends. I didn't like it but wear them I had to. As the saying goes, beggars can't be choosers and I suppose the reality was that we were little more than beggars. The other boots I had was a pair of button-up boots that were really awkward to do up, and that's putting it mildly. One side of the boot had six holes, the other side had matching buttons. To get the buttons through the holes a button-hook was employed, a long iron rod with a hook on the end. Putting the hook through the hole then round the button and pulling back through the hole was the method, six times for each boot. I just prayed and hoped that if Dad was going to get us some new clothes, it would include new footwear for me.

I can't remember ever having a new pair of shoes or boots, even in good times, as they were very expensive and we mostly relied on the many second-hand stalls in and around the Lane for our footwear. Once we had them they would last as long as possible and get repaired over and over again as long as there was still an ounce of life in them. These repairs were always carried out by Dad on a last he had, which had three foot sizes. The soles were always finished off with Blakey's metal studs, the heels having a half-round one at the back.

Dad replied, 'What about your friend, Ada? She's done all right for herself. How about asking her for a few cast-offs for the kids?' Ada Bloom was an old friend of Mum's, whom she had worked with at Toff Levy's. Ada had done all right for herself by marrying one of the bosses and had moved off to the leafy suburbs of Stamford Hill, living in her own house in the posh Osbaldeston Road. Ada had six or seven children of her own, varying in ages from a few years older than Julie, down to a two-year-old toddler, so there were plenty of clothes to be had.

The following day, the whole family went on an expedition to Stamford Hill. It was quite an adventure for us kids as we went on the tram. Although it didn't occur to me at the time, but thinking back now, I wonder where Dad got the money from for all the tram tickets. When we arrived at Osbaldeston Road itself I couldn't believe it. It was nothing like any road I had ever seen near where we lived.

I think I must have walked along this stunning quiet tree-lined street full of enormous Victorian houses with my jaw open all the way until we came to no. 95, Ada's house. There was a large knocker on the front door and Dad gave it a loud bash. Ada came to the door and looked a bit taken aback to see our motley crew on her doorstep. But her surprise soon gave way to a big smile, 'Becky, *bubbeleh*,' she said, beaming, and threw her arms round Mum. 'So lovely to see you. Come in, come in already!' As we went through the front door, I looked around her hallway and up the stairs and wondered how many families must be living here and where their rooms were.

She showed us in to her living room and once again my jaw dropped. I couldn't believe how big the room was. She sat us all down, with Mum and Dad sitting on a big leather sofa and us kids on the rest of the three-piece suite. The room contained a sideboard, a large gramophone, a huge table with six proper wooden chairs round it – not upside down crates – and an upright piano. I had never seen a room like this before. All this furniture! We would only have had just about enough room for the sofa in our house! Ada went off to the kitchen to rustle up some tea and cake. The cake was so delicious that I asked if there was any more. Mum immediately put her hands up, 'Oy vey, Ikey, where's your manners?' she said, 'I'm sorry about that, Ada.' Ada smiled and said, 'That's all right, of course he can have some more.' At which, Julie, David, Bill and Abie all started chorusing, 'Me, me too. I'd like some more cake.' I think Mum was a bit mortified as it looked as though she starved us, but Ada didn't seem to mind at all.

After tea and cake, Mum got to the point of the visit. 'Ada,' she began, 'I was wondering if you could help us out a bit. I wouldn't normally ask, but Jack's having a bit of a rough time at work, in fact there isn't much work and we haven't got a lot of money coming in. I was just hoping you might have some cast-off clothes from Clara, Rachel, Mossie and your other *kinder* that perhaps you don't need any more.'

'Of course, Becky,' smiled Ada, 'anything I can do to help. I'd be only too happy. You have such delightful children. So well-behaved.' And so we left Ada Bloom's with a sackful of children's clothes to sort out at home.

Over the next few years as Dad drifted in and out of work and both sets of children got bigger and bigger, this pilgrimage to Osbaldeston Road in Stamford Hill became something of a regular habit. But Ada never seemed to mind. In fact it was fairly general for the better-off to give their second-hand clothes away to poorer families. It was a bit like charity shops, only missing out the middleman and going straight from the donor to the needy.

We were fortunate enough after a few weeks of unemployment to have the gas man call. It was always a red-letter day when the gas man called, but especially if it came during one of Dad's periods of unemployment. The gas man unlocked and removed the money box, a heavy tin one, from the gas meter, spread the pennies out on the tabletop and started counting them into piles of twelve. Finishing this task, he then produced some five-shilling bank bags and put that amount of coins into each one. That accomplished, he put his share into a thick leather case and left us our rebate loose on the table. 'What a nice, kind man,' I said to Mum. 'Gertcha,' replied Mum, 'the old bugger's only left us what we've been overcharged anyway.'

This particular period of unemployment lasted several weeks, but with stale bread, cracked eggs, BMC tickets, cast-off clothes and the rest, we just about managed to struggle through. But I can still remember the day that Dad walked through the door and announced that one of the local cabinet makers, Solly Lebovsky, had offered him a French-polishing job. Mum broke down in tears again, but this time happy tears, and threw her arms round him. 'Oh Jack, that's wonderful.' Of course, there was an added reason for her joy this time as she knew by now that Manny was on his way.

This round of cracked eggs, stale bread, a penn'orth of jam, the Soup Kitchen and the Relieving Officer became a way of life for us for many years. Our only relief from this permanent pattern of poverty and living on charity came at Christmas and Easter as Dad could really only guarantee being in work as a French-polisher in the two months leading up to Christmas and for a month or so before Easter, when his skill was much in demand. At these times he would work late into the night earning as much money as he could to try to tide us over for a bit. We were always in bed by the time he got back home, but we went to sleep happy knowing that there would very likely be a little something for us in the morning as, on these occasions, he would always bring us home a little treat such as a bag of Everton Toffee or Sharps Kreemy Toffee, the latter always in a tin shaped like a bucket.

Christmas was eagerly anticipated by all us children. I doubt if our parents shared this enthusiasm but because Dad invariably was in work for the couple of months leading up to the big day, we didn't do too badly. A few weeks prior to this blessed event a cup was placed on the gas-meter shelf and we were told to put any money we might acquire from scavenging or doing odd jobs into it then, when we were asleep, Father Christmas would come and take it to help him get our presents. We followed this instruction to the letter as we couldn't take the risk of offending him of all people.

On Christmas Eve, Mum used to say to us, 'Don't forget to hang your stockings up. Father Christmas will be here during the night, then we can see which of you have been good boys and girls.' This was a bit worrying as we all started to remember some of the naughty things we had done during the year, but we hoped they would be outweighed by the good things we had done. So Christmas Eve saw a row of assorted stockings hanging from the mantelpiece, the younger members borrowing mum's stockings.

There was much anticipation the following morning as we all woke up early and there was a lot of chatter between us about what we might get and what we hoped for. We were always under strict instructions not to leave our room until Mum or Dad came in and told us it was time to get up. This waiting time was agony, which we usually tried to relieve by bouncing up and down on the beds and engaging in mock fights, much to Julie's disgust as she tried to quieten us down. Letting off steam like this not only tided us through the waiting time but helped keep us occupied and banish the lingering feeling we still had that we might have been too naughty to get any presents.

Eventually we were allowed up and we scampered into the living room where, to our great relief, we saw all the stockings filled. As we each dashed to our own stocking and opened it up the volume of the chatter would rise in crescendo as our excitement grew.

'I've got a tangerine,' Davy might say. 'Me too,' someone would add. Usually we found we all had oranges and some nuts and, if it was a particularly good Christmas, maybe even an apple or a tangerine. Having got through the fruit at the top, we would then start fishing out the little *schlorems* below. Now these were much more interesting than the foodstuff. And a typical Christmas continued like this:

'I've got some crayons,' came the cry from Bill. 'I've got some chalks,' said Abie, 'and a colouring book.' 'I've got one of those too,' put in Bill hurriedly, not wanting Abie to think he had more than him. 'I've got a story book,' I added to the list of presents being reported. 'What have you got, Julie?' I asked. Julie replied that she had a box of beads and a small paint tin. We all made little neat piles of our own presents and once that was complete, we'd go over to the table, for there on the table were some more presents with our names on.

'Look,' said Davy, 'I've got a Ludo game.' 'Well I've got snakes and ladders,' put in Abie. 'Lotto for me,' chimed in Bill. All of us had received a cheap board game or something similar. 'Mine's a Post Office,' I added. It contained little stamps and envelopes with some writing paper, a rubber stamp and some small weighing scales.

One year when I was a bit older I received a dartboard and three feather darts. The board was a square piece of laminated wood with a paper dartboard stuck on it. This must have been where my love of darts began, something I carried on into my young adult life.

Looking back from this distance of time, our presents were only cheap and nothing much to write home about but in relative terms they probably cost our parents an awful lot of money, though the sacrifice they must have made never entered our heads of course. After all, weren't all these presents from Father Christmas? In any case, to us our presents were simply wonderful and whether they were cheap or not we loved them because for the rest of the year there were hardly any treats. Even our birthdays went by without much, or even anything, by way of presents. Dad might be lucky and get a few weeks here and there, either as a French-polisher or a lino-cutter or as a waiter, but there were many more times when he was out of work than in it and we had to tighten our belts. It was a struggle just to put basic food on the table. Presents were completely out of the question. Of course, to me, growing up as young boy during this period, I didn't really think anything of it. I thought this must be how everyone lived.

After we'd opened all our presents we excitedly got down to the serious business of playing with them until dinner time, which although it was the normal chicken we might expect on a good Sunday, it was the only time of the year when we had roast chicken rather than boiled up for *lokshen* soup. With some roast potatoes and a bit of cabbage, it was the best meal of the year.

CHAPTER SIX

CIGARETTE CARDS, HORSE DUNG AND A TEN-BOB NOTE, 1919–26

'Can I have your cigarette card, please sir?' I asked in my most angelic voice. This was a regular refrain of mine as every time I saw someone open a packet of cigarettes, or a man smoking or taking a fag out of a box in the street, I'd run up to them and ask this all-important question. The answers varied from, 'Yeh, sure, 'ere you are.' to 'Piss off, kid!' On the whole I didn't do too badly.

As with most boys, cigarette cards or 'pitchers' as we called them amongst ourselves, became a bit of an obsession. The idea was to get a set – they generally came in sets of 25 or 50 – before your mates. Brand-new cards were worth five dirty ones, Sadly, the cards we generally played with in the street were dirty.

Cigarette cards were the poor child's encyclopaedia. They covered such a wide range of subjects, literature, sport, wild animals, ships and trains being just a few of the many. These small pieces of pasteboard had a great influence over my later life. They introduced me to Charles Dickens and those other two Victorian master craftsmen, Gilbert and Sullivan. The Dickens cards showed on the front a character and the novel he or she was to be found in, whilst giving on the back a brief account of the part that character played in the work, so whetting, at an early age, my appetite, now satiated, to know more about them.

The same thing went for the Gilbert and Sullivan characters; picture and opera on the front, synopsis on the back, making you want to know more about these people, these wonderful Savoyards. I have now seen all but two of these great works, the last two, *Utopia, Limited* and *The Grand Duke*, which, apart from the 1975 centenary, I don't think have been produced in my lifetime, at least not professionally.

Pinnace cigarettes, made by a local firm in Commercial Street, Godfrey Phillips, specialised in cards of footballers or cricketers in their packets. They were about half the size of the normal inserts and eagerly sought after by all the boys as they were real glossy photos. The numbers ran into hundreds so getting a set was almost impossible. I liked the cricketers best, especially the action photos, batsman at the crease or bowler running up.

There were quite a few different games we played with cigarette cards; some of the most popular were:

'Blowings'. This was played by placing the cards, all picture-side down, along a windowsill, lengthways. You'd spin a card to the ground to see who went first; if your guess was right, picture or back, when it landed you had first go. The first blower bent down and blew under his pack, one clean blow. As many as turned over to the picture side he kept. The first to blow his pack over could then in turn blow under the other pack, or what was left of it, keeping any blown over.

'Waterfalls'. A pitcher is held at an agreed height against the wall, the hand is removed and the card is allowed to flutter to the ground. This is done in turn until one card fully or partially covers another. The owner of the covering card then keeps all the pitchers that have accumulated on the ground.

'Flickings'. There is a variety of ways to play this game. Flick an agreed number of cards against the wall, nearest to the wall takes all. Lean a card against the wall about an inch out on the pavement, the first one to flick it down takes it and all the others that have tried and failed. Flick in turn to the wall and, as in 'Waterfalls', the card that rests on another takes all.

'Snap' was played in the conventional way using the last numeral of the card, i.e. 27 would be 7, 14 would be 4 etc. Turns were taken to put a card down, the second one to have the same number was the winner; there was no need to call 'Snap'.

Quite apart from cigarette cards I was an obsessive collector of practically any and everything. In particular I also collected bus and tram tickets of many and various colours and sizes, matchboxes and military-type buttons. These I obtained from Jack Lipschitz's workshop – fortunately he never found out! My real problem with all these collectibles was having somewhere to store them at home in our very limited space. Quite often I would return home after being out with my friends to find that Mum had binned the lot of them.

The reason I would be out in the street hunting down fag cards or playing with them was because, whether we had money or not, once any household chores were finished, Mum would always shoo us outside into the street and tell us to play out there as long as it wasn't raining too hard. A little drizzle we could put up with. The same scenes were repeated all along the street as the mothers threw the kids out of the house, so at the weekend, during holidays and after school, the street was crowded with children of all ages trying to play different games. Apart from pitchers, the most popular boys' game was leapfrog. We used to play this up and down the street getting in everybody's way, especially if a large number took part. Another popular game was rolling hoops along. Practically every child had a hoop of some description and boys and girls vied with each other for the available space as children steered them up and down the overloaded street. For every shop-bought hoop there would be a dozen improvised ones. Large pram or bicycle wheels were favourite, but many a smaller one would also be pressed into service.

Peg tops was another popular game but mainly for boys. These came in various woods and sizes. The best ones were called boxers because they were made from boxwood and therefore very tough. Wide at the top and tapering down to a metal peg, they had a very close groove running all the way down to the peg. By winding a thin cord around the groove from bottom to top you were ready to spin it. Holding the top and cord tightly in one hand, the arm would be raised above the shoulder and the top thrown to the ground, leaving the thrower holding the cord. If all went well, as the top unwound itself from the cord it would start spinning and continue to do so at a very fast rate on hitting the ground. There was of course a knack in the way the top was thrown; many a time it would hit the ground, bounce, then lie still. When they were spinning fast we'd put our hand under them and scoop them up and they would continue spinning on our palm.

Whipping tops were widespread too. These were sort of mushroom-shaped – flat top and a wide, straight stem. They were made from common white wood with a small peg at the bottom. They were spun with the fingers then whipped to keep them going. A good exponent of this art could send the top yards up the street with just one good whip.

Various ball games were played by boys and girls. One was hitting the wall via the pavement and catching it on its return, counting each time you caught it, while a slightly harder version was to place a flat object on the pavement, preferably a coin, and you only counted when you hit the object. Football and cricket were for the boys. The wicket was anything you could find; a box was ideal. We only played one end; double wickets were for the professionals.

The venue for these games was generally Shepherd Street because Palmer Street, with its younger children playing around and their mothers sitting outside gossiping and eating monkey nuts, was much too narrow and overcrowded for good stroke play, while Shepherd Street, being longer and wider and not so busy, could well give the Jack Hobbs within a chance to show himself, even though the bat may well have been fashioned from a piece of the ubiquitous orange box. Football was played at the same venue. The main opposition we were always up against was not the other team but the people who lived in the street and the local bobby who were forever trying to move us on. Did they not want any future International or Test stars? One adult, though, who did quite well out of our playing these ball games in the street was Myer Kutner, the local glazier, as many a time was he called out to repair a broken window resulting from some overenthusiastic kicking or batting.

The girls had their own ball games and always sang as they played them; 'One, two, three, O'Leary', 'Aunt Sally Sells Fish' are two I remember. The latter song was also sung when skipping. All girls seemed to have a skipping rope, if not an official one with two wooden handles, then at least a long measure of cord. They would skip singly, in pairs or in multiples. When they skipped in pairs one girl would start on her own, singing of course, and during the song would invite another girl in. As soon as this girl saw her chance she would go in, picking up the step, facing the girl who had called her. When they all played, two girls would take an end of the rope each and as they started to turn the rope the inevitable song would begin, a few well-remembered ones being 'On a Mountain Stands a Lady', 'In and Out the Windows' and 'Rosie Apple Lemonade Tart'. All the girls would be invited to skip in one by one till eventually, if it went well, they would all be skipping in a long line.

Higher and Higher was a rope game enjoyed by boys and girls together. Like multiple skipping, the rope would be held at each end and pulled taut; the remainder would line up in front in single file, about a yard or so away. On the word 'Go' they would all jump over the rope and return to where they started. If you didn't jump the new height you fell out. Each time a round was completed off they'd go again, only for each new round the rope was raised till finally there would be only one jumper left.

Marbles and Gobs was another game for all, but girls were more adept at it. It was played with five cube-like stones ribbed down each side from top to bottom and a large stone marble. It was never my cup of tea.

Hopscotch was another game girls excelled at. A chalk hopscotch would be drawn out on the pavement. The pattern was two squares at the bottom, one square above and in the middle of these, then two more above that one, then one again and finally two in an arched top. Each square was numbered; the game was to kick a chipper into each box whilst hopping. That wasn't for me either.

Diabolo was played by the older girls. A diabolo looked like a very large cotton reel tapered sharply from each side to the centre. It was spun round on a string held by two wooden handles. When it was spinning fast enough it was thrown in the air and caught again on the string then relaunched skyward again. This could go on for quite a while if you were an expert.

Although we spent most of our day out in the street when not at school, they were not exactly the healthiest of places to play in. Dogs roamed about in packs leaving their trademark anywhere and everywhere, add to this the contribution made by the horses and it was, to say the least, not an ideal environment. In the summer the water cart and road sweeper did their best to clean things up a bit but they fought a losing battle. The dustcart came round I suppose once a week. It was like a long, deep, oblong box on wheels, horse-drawn. It had steps, a kind of ladder, at the back. The dustmen had long, leather hats down to the back of their necks and wore some sort of corduroy trousers strapped just below the knee.

Another popular place to play was Butler Street. From the Duke of Wellington pub on the corner with Shepherd Street, running the whole length of the street to Tenter Street, was a row of completely ruined houses. These were like a magnet to us and we would run around in their ruins, playing hide and seek, tag and just generally jumping up and down over the wreckage. They were just left in this state for many years, and, of course, at that time no one thought to cordon them off as being dangerous, though many's the cut and bruise that was suffered in there through falling on to broken glass or other sharp edges. As far as I can remember there were never any more serious injuries, but that was probably more through luck than anything else.

Naturally at the time I never thought to consider why there was a row of ruined houses there but thinking about it now, I guess they must have been rendered so during one of the many air raids Spitalfields suffered during the Great War, probably on the night of 13 June 1917, when two Gothas dropped their bombs in that vicinity, killing close to 100 people and injuring 500 more. It is a matter of record that Nathanial Buildings, about 30 yards across the way from Butler Street in Flower and Dean Street had many of its flats damaged in that raid.

As well as the street games we all played I had a few adventures all of my own. Most of the time, in keeping with my responsibilities as the oldest boy, I was charged with looking after my younger brothers so I didn't always get much time to myself. There were some occasions when I managed to get away from them, however. One of these times when I was alone, I decided for reasons I cannot now remember to pick up a small dog and swing it around by its tail. I shudder when I think of this appalling and inexcusable episode today. Anyway, I was in mid-swing when Uncle Woolfy turned into the street.

'Ikey!' he bellowed. I was so surprised I let the dog go sharply and it flew several yards up the street, fortunately landing on its feet. 'What do you think you're doing?' he continued. 'I'll tell your father!' I ran off and was dreading going home that night. Although Dad wasn't a great one for smacking or slapping, there were occasions when he would give out the odd right-hander if he felt it was deserved. I was sure that this was one of those times when he would feel it was deserved. However, as it happened, I heard no more of the incident. I suspect Uncle Woolfy had forgotten all about it by the time he saw Dad.

On another occasion however, I wasn't quite so lucky in escaping retribution. This was the time that I saw a pile of horse shit in the middle of the road outside Hester Woolf's house – nothing unusual about that of course. This time the dung was shaped like little round balls and as her top window was down, I picked these little balls up and threw them one at a time through the window. Having done that I made my way towards Shepherd Street chuckling to myself. Suddenly, somebody grabbed me from behind and rubbed a load of horse shit in my mouth and all over my face. 'Serves you right,' came a voice from behind me. By the time I'd stopped choking and spluttering enough to turn round and face my attacker he'd gone, so I never did know who had done it.

'*Oy gevalt*, Ikey, what the bleedin' 'ell's happened to you already?' Mum said when I reached home. Shamefacedly, I told her what I'd done and what had happened. 'You stupid little bugger,' she said, without any sympathy at all. 'Go and get a pail of water.' After Mum had poured the water into the sink, she gave my face a good hard rub with Lifebuoy – harder than I think she need have done, but I was in no position to complain. Once I was cleaned up to her satisfaction, she gave me a quick clip round the ear and sent me out again. 'Don't you ever do anything like that again,' she warned. I never did.

On another occasion, I was watching a man selling live chickens in nearby Cobb Street. This was quite a normal thing then. They were housed in wooden boxes made with slats and with a lid on top for taking out the chosen bird. The boxes were on a stall. I noticed a chicken lying on the ground under the stall. 'Please, mister,' I said, pointing to the bird, 'there's a chicken under your stall.' The man looked and said, much to my surprise, 'So there is, sonny, would you like it?' I did a double take. For some reason I had always wanted a chicken of my own, though I had no idea where I would keep it. I managed to keep calm and just said, 'Yes please, sir, I'd love it.' I picked it up and tucked it under my arm feeling very pleased with myself.

When I got home Dad was there. He looked at me and my chicken with a mixture of shock and suspicion and, although not usually given to using the more extreme swear words, especially in front of us children, the incongruous sight of me with a chicken under my arm got the better of him and he blurted out, 'What the fuck have you got there? Where did you get it from?' 'I got it from a man in Cobb Street,' I told him. 'He said I could have it.' After he'd got over his initial shock, Dad took a look at the bird and shook his head, 'No wonder he let you have it, it's not moving, something's wrong with it.' Which was true. 'I'd better take it over to Mottle,' he said. Mottle Simons was a friend of Dad's who kept a few fowl in his yard. So Dad, the sickly chicken and I went round to see Mottle, whose exact words, after taking one look at it, were, 'I don't give much for its chances.' However, he said he would see what he could do. And that was the last I ever saw or heard of my chicken.

That wasn't the only trophy I brought home that shocked my parents. Mooching along Bell Lane one day I saw a ten-shilling note at my feet. Now that was real money! I picked it up and ran all the way home with it in great excitement. As soon as I got it indoors, I waved it triumphantly in front of Mum and said, 'Look what I just found.'

However, instead of being welcomed with open arms, I was immediately interrogated. 'Where the soddin' 'ell d'you get that from?' she said.

'I found it on the pavement in Bell Lane,' I said excitedly.

'Are you sure?' she asked.

'Yes,' I said, a bit disappointed that I seemed to be being treated like a criminal rather than the hero I thought I was. When I finally assured her she said, 'Did anyone see you pick it up?' I shook my head. 'Did anyone follow you home?' she persisted. Again I shook my head.

During the whole of this conversation, Mum kept looking out of the window as though expecting the police to call at any minute. Finally I was cleared of wrongdoing and of being seen or followed and Mum took the note. 'Don't you dare say a word about this to anyone, Ikey,' she said before ushering me out again. So much for finding a ten-bob note, I thought, perhaps next time I'll leave it where it is!

However, I noticed we did eat rather well for the rest of that week.

When I was a bit older I would sometimes go off for walks completely away from the Tenterground just to get away and be entirely on my own. Mostly my route on those occasions took me up Mansell Street as far as Tower Bridge, passing the Royal Mint. The Mint had a low wall with high railings along its front. On the other side of the railings was a square pond with goldfish. Many times on entering Mansell Street I would see flocks of sheep being driven into what must have been an abattoir.

CHAPTER SEVEN

CATS' MEAT, CATCH 'EM ALIVE AND PERCY THE HOOK, 1919–26

Vying with all the children playing out in the street, many itinerant vendors and tradesmen would try to make their living by calling round the streets during the day.

There was the cats' meat man, with his basket of canine and feline goodies on his arm – lean meat on a skewer for the cats; rough, consisting of all the gristly bits, for the dogs – and the legendary muffin man, renowned in nursery rhyme for living down Drury Lane, tray on head always covered by a white cloth, ringing his hand bell to proclaim his presence to addicts of this toothsome delicacy.

The vendor of hearthstone, salt and vinegar used a barrow to cart his wares about. Hearthstone was used indoors for whitening the hearth, thus making a fine contrast to the stove and oven, which would be blackleaded. Salt was always sawn off a large block to the required amount. I always remember it as triangular. For vinegar you handed him your own bottle which he filled from a keg.

The watercress man was patronised on Sunday as it went well with Dutch herrings in a sandwich. If, owing to the state of the exchequer that week, there were no Dutch herrings, well, it made a nice sandwich on its own.

A man used to come round selling apples from a homemade handcart; a box, two wheels and a pair of wooden shafts nailed to the sides. He had a wooden leg, no doubt a victim of the war trying to keep body and soul together.

Occasionally the lavender girl would appear, basket on arm, singing the centuries-old song 'Won't You Buy My Sweet Blooming Lavender?', and in it telling how many branches she was selling for a penny. The stuff used to give me a headache so I always ran inside as soon as I heard her voice.

Travelling tinkers and chair menders were other Wheatley throwbacks; the latter repaired cane and raffia chairs. (Note: The painter Francis Wheatley created a well-known series of oil paintings known as 'Cries of London', which depicted all these old travelling street sellers. These were exhibited at the Royal Academy between 1792 and 1795 and were turned into engravings; there have been prints made of these paintings many times ever since. My dad loved them and we had a number of copies of the prints hanging up in our house for many years.)

'Scissors or knives to grind' had a three-wheeled barrow. A can of water above the grindstone gave a steady drip as he plied his craft.

The flypaper man did a good trade in the summer months,

especially the hot ones. His cry as he entered the street was 'Catch 'em alive'. In those days flies in summertime were almost a plague; they were everywhere, bluebottles, greenbottles, big flies, little flies and many other types of fly. The flypaper was in appearance like a fat shotgun cartridge with a tab one side and a loop the other. When the tab was pulled it unfurled into a long strip of celluloid-looking paper covered with a brown, treacly-looking substance. When this was hung up in the room by the door it attracted flies by the score to a sticky end.

'All the latest songs' was another now-and-then visitor. He sold a song sheet like a six-page tabloid, no music, just the lyrics, verse and refrain. I don't know how many songs it contained, and as for being all the latest, that depended on what you called the latest.

Occasionally the odd hawker and pedlar selling bootlaces or matches might put in an appearance, but they generally kept to the Lane. They had a tray in front supported by two shoulder straps. Many displayed signs saying they were unable to work due to wartime injuries and had wives and children to support. Heroes, no doubt, but poor ones trying to eke out a crust in a land that wasn't really fit for them after all.

Poppy was the name of our local paper boy. Boy being a bit of a misnomer as I suppose he was about forty to fifty years old. He would first appear in the street about midday calling out 'All the runners and riders'. Interest in papers in the Tenterground centred on horse racing. I do believe most people thought Steve Donoghue was the Prime Minister rather than Stanley Baldwin or Ramsey MacDonald.

During the afternoon Poppy would be back at about hourly

intervals with the latest results, printed in the stop press column of the midday editions. Late afternoon or evening he would be back with the *Final Star*, the most popular paper. This would contain all the day's racing results.

When he wasn't running round the streets bringing glad tidings to the punters, he would station himself on the corner of White's Row. The earliest headline I can remember posted up on one of his placards proclaimed in thick black letters 'Bonar Law Dead.'

There were also several merchants who used horse-drawn carts as their form of transport. The most popular with me was 'N. Laid, Mineral Water'. When we had money we would avail ourselves of his service. His drinks came in crates of a dozen or half-dozen, but, of course, if you couldn't afford a full crate you could buy as many as you liked. The crates contained a variety of drinks – cola, lemonade and cream soda were our favourites.

Then there was Marriage and Impey, sterilised milk purveyors. The cart had a large sterilised milk bottle painted on each of its sides in the form of a gentleman with the caption 'Madam I am Pure'. These bottles had an unusual method of opening them; a metal bar attached to each side of the stopper had to be pushed up to open it and down to close.

The other horse drawn salesman was Reckitt Smith, coal merchant. He sold his coal in made-up sacks of a hundredweight and half-hundredweight. His call of 'Coalman' was heard regularly in the winter. When the kitty wouldn't stand a hundredweight of coal from Reckitt Smith I would be sent to one of two oil shops for 7 lb or 14 lb of coal in a bucket, either

Hyams in Bell Lane or a shop-cum-shed affair in Tenter Street, just past Butler Street. The scales in which the coal was weighed were enormous; I expect they weighed a hundredweight or more themselves. Getting 7 lb back home wasn't too bad, but 14 lb weighed a ton, if you see what I mean. To supplement this meagre amount of fuel, the Lane and Spitalfields Market would be scoured for any wooden boxes lying about.

Two ice-cream vendors came around when the weather was favourable for that commodity. One had a smart, posh barrow, nicely painted. It contained two freezers, one for vanilla the other for lemon ice. This was crushed ice with some lemon flavour added. Both were sold between wafers or in cornets. This gentleman was called Johnny, but weren't they all? As soon as he appeared on the scene the cry would go up 'Give us a taster, Johnny.' I got quite a few in my time, always lemon ice, never vanilla.

The other purveyor of cold delicacies had an ordinary barrow with one freezer in the middle. Two large placards, one each side of the freezer, informed us that this was 'The original Joe Assenheim's of 56 Stepney Lane'. No tasters here; more likely a thick ear. This ice cream was sold in oblong shapes wrapped in plain white paper, half strawberry and half cream. They cost tuppence whole, penny half. The half was always cut on the diagonal so that you got both strawberry and cream.

Hot-chestnut and hot-potato vendors were plentiful in the winter months. These merchants also plied their wares from handcarts on which stood a portable coke fire with a grill over the top to cook these cold weather luxuries.

As if all this activity in the street wasn't enough, there was quite a variety of street entertainers knocking about, all trying to earn a crust, or, at least, enough for a pint. Street singers were by far the commonest, after all anybody could sing, or nearly anybody. Mind you there were some good ones about too. Like most of the pedlars, many would have a sign fixed to their chest, the commonest again being 'Disabled, unable to work, wife and children to support.' People playing instruments were not uncommon: cornets, fiddles, mouth organs, concertinas and Jews' harps to name a few.

There was a most unusual act came down the street one day. Four or five people in eighteenth-century costume – knee breeches, stockings, yellow wigs on their heads, silver buckles on their shoes. I believe they were all men but I can't be sure. They were accompanied by a barrel organ, the organist dressed in the same style. The players lined up in front of the organ and when it commenced to play they did a sort of tap dance on the spot. When it stopped they struck a pose, a tableau, holding it till the organ played again when they started to tap dance again until the organ stopped when they held a different scene. The tableau I remember to this day was one man about to stab another but having his arm held by a third man. I've often wondered since how they could have lived on the odd coppers they received. They certainly needed better pitches than Palmer Street.

Old Solomon Levi was a very well-known character in the area. I don't think that was his name; we called him that because of the song he always sang. 'Old Solomon Levi Keeps a Clothes Shop in the Lane'. I have forgotten most of it because the rest was in Yiddish. He would march round the streets followed by all us kids, singing and playing a kazoo. He was one of the sights of the Lane, especially on Sunday mornings.

The two most popular entertainers were Harry Lawson and Percy the Hook, both of whom were frequent visitors and returned time after time in spite of all the abuse that came their way.

Harry Lawson would come into the street strumming a banjo and singing his own compositions, the most famous being 'Bring the Night Po', a sad song indeed about a man who did the inevitable in the bed because he was too ill to get up and his wife brought the po too late. Every time he put in an appearance he copped out; flour was poured over his head, an egg cracked into it and rubbed in, another time soot instead of flour. The people doing this were not children but grown men. Despite the treatment he received he carried on strumming and singing, everybody laughing, including Harry himself. It would finally end when one of the women took him in and attempted to clean him up. The men would then have a whip round for him and off he'd go to pastures new.

Percy the Hook was a barrel-organ operator. He wore very thick glasses. It was said he suffered from fits. When he arrived we all gathered round his organ and, as soon as he started to play, a continuous chant of 'Percy the Hook, Percy the Hook' would go up. When he'd had enough he would shout back, 'Sod off, you little buggers.' As the baiting continued he'd go into full screaming mode and his language would get worse and worse. The more he screamed and swore the louder we'd chant, till, with a final, 'Piss off, you bunch of fucking wankers,' he'd take the handle from his barrel organ and chase us up the street with it. Why he kept coming back to go through this again and again I have no idea! He must have been doing it for some years too, because Mum once told me that she danced round his organ when she was a little girl.

The rain didn't stop any of this activity going on. We would still be turfed out to play in the streets, the visiting tradespeople and entertainers would still come round. In fact, the street was even more cluttered on rainy days as many people put their aspidistras out in the street to be watered by this natural process. So everyone had to weave their way in and out around all the pots on the ground. The aspidistra was the standard house plant. Everyone seemed to possess one. Even we, in our parlous financial position, had one.

The only time all this activity stopped during the daytime was on Armistice Day. Once a year at the eleventh hour of the eleventh day of the eleventh month the maroon fireworks would go off and the two minutes' silence the sound heralded was rigidly observed by everyone. All the traffic stopped and people would stand still. Many people were, of course, still grieving for loved ones lost in the conflict whom they would never see again. For such people the war would never be over. Ex-service men proudly wore their medals, some from the Boer War, as there were still a lot of soldiers from that older war around as well. Many, from both wars, were now sadly reduced to scrabbling around in the gutters for dog ends as their reward for loyal service, once the maroons sent them on their way again.

CHAPTER EIGHT

MALT, HENNY PENNY AND SWEET STUFF SHOPS, 1920–6

One morning, I must have been about four at the time, Dad said to me, 'Come on, Ikey, get your coat on, we're going with Julie this morning.' I thought that was a bit strange because Julie was going to school, as she had been doing for the last year or so. Well, it soon became clear to me why I was going with Julie, it was because I too was going to school, the Jews Infant School, situated about a minute's walk from my house. To reach it Dad took us through a narrow opening on the corner of Shepherd Street and Tilley Street which opened into a small square with the school gate opposite. To the immediate right of the wall was a cowshed with six or eight cows. In the wall to the far right was a small dairy called Barker's which sold warm milk to the schoolchildren. On this particular morning, Dad bought Julie and me a glass. They cost a ha'penny each.

Passing Barker's, a small alley ran on into the Lane, with, on one corner, Ostwind's the baker, and, on the other, a tobacconist I was to get to know well over the years as I would often be sent there for half an ounce of light shag and a packet of AG fag papers for Dad.

On arriving, Julie skipped off to her class, while Dad and I were greeted by a tall man wearing a smart suit and tie, who I later learned was the headmaster, Mr Unckly. He shook Dad's hand and said, 'Good to meet you again, Mr Jacobs; so this is young Isaac, is it?' Dad nodded in agreement and with that Mr Unckly propelled me off across the playground with a sharp shove in the back, saying, 'Up the stairs at the end.' I walked off alone, trying to feel brave, but feeling quite wretched inside. I knew Julie went to school, but I didn't really know what it meant, and here I was all alone. I looked behind me and saw Dad walking off out the school gates. An empty feeling spread through me and I had no idea what to expect. At the end of the playground was the flight of steps the strange man who had met me at the entrance had told me to go up, so up I went. After three steps the stairs came into another playground with a long row of bench seating along one side and, on a bracket protruding from the wall to its right, was a large bell, which I was later to learn was Mr Unckly's pride and joy, which he rang at the beginning of school, at the end of school and at all points in between.

To the left was another flight of stairs leading up, so I continued climbing and finally came into a room set out with rows of desks, a big table at the front and a large blackboard on an easel. Strangely though, it was out in the open air. There were already a number of children about my age and older sitting at some of the desks with a well-dressed woman sitting at the table. As I looked in the class, she said, without looking up, 'Come in. Name?' I assumed she was asking my name, so I said, 'Ikey.' The other children all laughed and I wondered what was so funny about the name Ikey. The woman looked up and smiled. 'No,' she said. 'What's your full name?' 'Oh, er, Isaac Jacobs,' I spluttered. 'Thank you, Isaac,' she said. 'Now take your boots off and place them in that cupboard.' She pointed to a large cupboard at the back of the room. 'You'll find a space with your name written on it –' which was a bit pointless as I couldn't read yet – 'and then find a seat.'

Take my boots off!? I could feel myself going red. As usual, my socks had a couple of enormous holes in them. I wasn't expecting this. However, I felt I couldn't argue with this woman, so I slowly removed them trying to hide the holes as best I could by twisting my feet at strange angles. I quickly found a seat towards the back of the room as this saved me from having to walk far and let everyone see my socks.

A few more children arrived and went through the same introduction. When we were all ready, the woman stood up and said, 'Good morning.' Silence. 'When I say good morning, you all say "Good morning, ma'am." Let's try again.' This time we got it right and she smiled. 'Good,' she continued. 'My name is Miss Solomons and I am your teacher. If you behave and work hard you will find me a very nice lady, but if you play up or slack, you will find me a very nasty lady. Is that clear?' A few children nodded. 'No,' she said. 'You say, "yes ma'am!"' So we all dutifully nodded and said, 'Yes, ma'am.' All this ma'aming was very new to me as it obviously was to everyone else. But she seemed quite a nice woman, I thought and so it turned out. She was true to her word and if you got on with your work and didn't play up, she was, as she said, 'a very nice lady'.

So after a bit of a difficult start, the morning was just about to get a whole lot better, as the next thing that happened was we were all given a spoonful of malt, something I had never experienced before, but it tasted wonderful, just like toffee. We were given this first thing every morning. It certainly encouraged you to get to school on time.

After malt, the next thing we did was to begin learning the alphabet. We were all given some small yellow cardboard squares with one large black letter written on each one. Miss Solomons then held one up and said, 'A' or whatever was written on it. Our job was to find the card with the same shape on it and hold it up as well. Once she was satisfied that we all had the right card, she said, 'A,' again, and then added, 'Now you say it.' Obediently, we all chorused, 'A'. This went on for several days until we could recognise all the letters. The next step was to put two or three together to make words, eventually leading to us being able to read and write.

After doing this for some time, Miss Solomons told us to put our letters away and gave out some small wooden boxes with a lid that slid off between two grooves along the top. Inside were some different shaped building blocks. Once again, Miss Solomons would hold one up and say, 'Triangle,' and we followed the same procedure as with the letter cards. These blocks were quite fun, but I suppose they were our introduction to geometry; thinking about it all these years later, it seems a bit strange that we went straight into that before learning numbers.

At twelve o'clock, Mr Unckly rang his bell and we were all allowed home for lunch. Julie and I were met at the school gate by Mum, along with the rest of the Jacobs children, and walked back home. We had to return by two for afternoon school, but, strangely enough, there were no lessons and, as soon as we got back, it was boots off again and we had to get into our collapsible beds, which had mysteriously appeared in our classroom. These consisted of two wooden ends with a string hammock slung between them. We were told to get into them and that we were to go to sleep. This seemed very strange to me as I had grown out of sleeping in the afternoon some time ago. Not only was I not tired, but the string in the hammock bit into my legs – of course we all wore short trousers at that age – and was very uncomfortable. Even if I had wanted to go to sleep I don't think I would have been able to. And so passed a very boring ninety minutes. At three-thirty, we were told to get up and to come down the front of the class and sit on the floor in a semi-circle round Miss Solomons, who proceeded to tell us a story until home time at four o'clock.

The first story she ever told us was about Henny Penny and it scared the life out of me for a long time afterwards. In the story Miss Solomons told, an acorn from a very tall oak tree fell on Henny Penny's head, which led her to believe the sky was falling in, so she decided to go and warn the king, meeting many other birds and animals on the way, who all followed her to the palace. As she read the story, Miss Solomons passed round the book to show us the illustrations. It was the picture of the tall tree nearly bumping into the sky that caught my attention as very close to where I lived there was a small park called Itchy Park, which contained three very tall trees just like the one in the drawing. For months afterwards I would eye these trees very suspiciously for any sign that they were bumping into the sky and causing it to fall in. It was a constant worry to me!

Sometimes, instead of a story, she would teach us to sing nursery rhymes. The first nursery rhyme I remember was 'Simple Simon'.

After that first day, mornings would always start with morning assembly. This took place in the hall downstairs. Prayers were in Hebrew, so I didn't understand a word of them.

And so every day followed this pattern of assembly, malt and lessons until lunch at midday, back at two, then sleep, stories or nursery rhymes and home at four-thirty. The only exception to this came on Fridays when assembly was followed by singing lessons. These were taken by another teacher, a Miss Harris, who accompanied us on the piano. Songs that come readily to mind are 'I had a Little Nut Tree', 'At Concord Stable Stands a Tree' and 'London Bridge is Falling Down'.

The other big change on Fridays was that school only lasted from nine to two-thirty, with a much shorter lunch break and no sleep in the afternoon. We called this 'Double Lessons' day. The reason for this shorter day was to enable the children to be home before dark, especially in the winter, so we could all celebrate the Sabbath, which begins at dusk on Friday.

One day, not long after I started, Mum woke me up to get ready for school, but I didn't feel very well. 'Mum,' I said. 'Do

I have to go?' Mum looked at me and said, 'Of course you do, Ikey. What made you ask already?' 'I don't feel well,' I replied. Mum took a look at me and felt my forehead to see if I had a temperature. By this time Julie and Davy were both awake; Julie was getting ready for school herself and said, 'Come on, Ikey, we'll be late.' But Mum said, 'No, you do feel a bit hot and you look a bit pasty. Have you got a pain?' 'I've got a really bad headache, Mum,' I said. Davy laughed and put in, 'You're just trying to get out of school.' 'No, Mum,' I protested. 'I really don't feel well.' 'It's OK, Ikey,' Mum said reassuringly, 'I think you'd better stay off school today and see how it goes.' She then shooed Julie and Davy outside. Which was just as well, because just as they left the room, I was suddenly sick all over the bed. '*Oy gevalt*, Ikey,' Mum said, leaping back out of range. 'You definitely need to stay off.'

This was the first time I had one of these episodes, but from then on, for a number of years, I suffered these bilious attacks which manifested themselves by a splitting headache over my left eye and vomiting on and off throughout the day. By nightfall I was invariably fit and well again, and hungry, having had nothing to eat all day.

After about the fifth or sixth time this happened over the course of about a year, our doctor sent me to the infirmary in Vallance Road a few times but as this was between attacks, they couldn't find out what was wrong, so they decided to keep me in under observation and did a few tests. After a few days they sent for Dad to come and get me. Their verdict was that there was nothing fundamentally wrong with me and I that would grow out of the attacks. They were right, I did eventually. But for the next couple of years I continued to suffer them on and off, gradually decreasing in regularity.

Another hospital job round about that time was having my tonsils out. This deed was done in Gray's Inn Road Ear, Nose and Throat Hospital. I'll never forget that kidney-shaped dish I was sick in, all blood, whilst sitting on Dad's lap after the event. It was a very scary experience. After a while it was the tram back to Commercial Street and carried home to bed, towel over my mouth and a few more days off school.

Strangely enough, although ours was a strictly Jewish school, everybody in class received a present at Christmas. These were laid out on a table and as our teacher called a name that child went to the table and selected one. I can well remember once having my eye on a set of skittles, little wooden ones with a ball in the middle tied round with string. After what seemed like ages it was my turn. The skittles, still unclaimed, were mine. Exactly the same thing happened the following year, by which time I had lost all my skittles from the previous year. So, same waiting ordeal then my turn. Once again I was the proud owner of a set of skittles.

Eventually, when I was seven, the time came to go to the big school, the Jews' Free School. The older boys in the street would tell about how strict the masters were and how they made frequent use of the cane both on your knuckles and on your bottom. At the infants, apart from the headmaster, Mr Unckly, we only had teachers; we used the term master and teacher to denote male and female, so I had never really experienced a master before. To get to school I followed a narrow alley which commenced where Tilley Street and Tenter

Street met. This went right through to Bell Lane emerging opposite Cobb Street. Halfway through this alley on the left-hand side was another cowshed, longer than the one by the infant school. It probably belonged to Barker too. There were three entrances to the school; Middlesex Street, Strype Street and Bell Lane.

On my first morning, I was shown where my classroom was. This time the school was strictly segregated into boys and girls, so my class was boys only. I was quite worried about what sort of master I would have and, although I had pretended not to take any notice of the older boys' tales about the masters, they did prey on my mind. As it turned out, I had absolutely no need to worry at all. After we had all taken our places a rather pleasant older man strode into the class and said, 'Good morning, boys.' Of course, by now, we had all learnt to say, 'Good morning, sir.' 'My name is Mr Rosenthal,' he announced as our voices trailed away, 'and I will be your teacher.' The first thing I noticed about him was that he had a big white moustache. Like Miss Solomons before him, he told us that if we worked hard and didn't give him any cheek, we would find him 'more your friend than a master', but if we played up in any way, woe betide us! He then explained a bit about school and what we would be doing. And so my first morning at 'big school' passed quite uneventfully and, I have to say, quite pleasantly. This Mr Rosenthal didn't seem like the cane-swishing ogre I had imagined in the least.

When lunchtime came, I went home for a slice of bread and marge, which was to become a daily habit. There was a tuckshop in one of the playgrounds but, alas, I don't remember putting any business its way. I could never afford anything.

When I did get home that first lunchtime, naturally, Mum and Dad (who was in one of his out-of-work periods) asked me how I'd got on. I told them that my teacher seemed all right and that his name was Mr Rosenthal. Dad suddenly spluttered and started coughing. He looked as though he was about to choke on his cigarette. Finally he managed to blurt out, 'Rosey?' 'Are you all right, Dad?' I said. 'Has he got a big white moustache?' he asked. 'Yes,' I replied. After getting over his choking fit, Dad then started laughing. 'Well I'll be jiggered,' he said, 'Old Rosey Rosenthal. He was my bloody teacher as well. My God! He must be getting on a bit.'

The school was divided into two departments: Intermediate School, headmaster Mr Michaels, and the Central School, headmaster Mr Bowman. The Central School was for the elite, the clever boys. They wore a yellow ring round the middle of their caps, which we always referred to as a *beigel*. Sadly I never felt as though I could aspire to wear one of those beigels and I knew that my parents couldn't wait for me to reach the age of fourteen so I could leave school and go out and earn some money. They weren't really interested in academic achievement and therefore nor was I. Looking back now, of course, it was a great shame that we were driven into those feelings by force of circumstances as I actually liked school, especially English Literature and History. In other times and other circumstances I like to think I could have made a go of school and gone on past my fourteenth birthday and, who knows, maybe even attain some sort of qualifications. But all the kids I knew were in the same boat as me and, no matter how clever any of us might be, none of us ever stood a chance.

There were many out-of-school activities provided. In the evenings for example, there was a chess club which I joined and I got to be reasonably good at the game. There was also a Hebrew class, though I didn't join it. Later on, my brother Abie joined and became the only member of our family able to speak the ancient language of our race.

Football and cricket were always popular and we had plenty of space to play these as the school possessed no less than four playgrounds. There was also a boxing ring set up in the school hall after hours for those wishing to partake of this sport. It looked too painful to me, so I decided to stick to chess.

Our school was also noted for its band, the Jewish Lads' Brigade. Every evening when they were at practice in the school playground, the sound would echo all round the Tenterground. 'Semper Fidelis' is the tune I'll always remember them for.

When school was over, on the rare occasions Dad was in work and I had some pocket money on me, I might be tempted to look in one of the sweet shops on the way home. We were lucky enough to have five sweet shops, or, as Mum called them, sweet stuff shops, all within a few seconds' walk of our house. Well, shop is a bit grandiose as they were in fact front rooms of houses converted to sell a few sweets.

Martha Wakeman ran one, selling a few other items one might need in the house as well. On the outside wall was a big tinplate sign, yellow with black lettering that read 'Colman's DSF Mustard'. I would rack my brain trying to decipher DSF without any success. Neither friends nor family could help. Even Martha Wakeman herself had no idea what it meant. What on earth could DSF stand for and what did it have to do with mustard? It was a real puzzler. It wasn't until about fifty years later, whilst watching television, that I saw an advert singing the praises of 'Colman's double superfine mustard' that I finally realised what DSF stood for. As I always say, you're never too old to learn.

At the end of the street Mrs Cohen sold cheap games and novelties as well as sweets: board games like snakes and ladders, and bombs, the latter, mainly for boys, consisted of two pieces of metal which, when put together, formed a bomb shape, held together by a string with a loop knot at the top. The bomb had four grooves running down its side for the string to hold it firm. To operate this weapon, the string was slackened, some caps inserted between the two halves, and the string tightened, drawing the two halves together. The bomb was then primed and ready. The idea was that when thrown up in the air it would return to earth with a loud bang as the caps exploded.

For the girls there were dolls and dresses which were pressed out of a sheet of cardboard. The doll could be dressed by bending four tabs, one on each corner of the dress, round its back. Shoes and hats working on this tab system also came with the card.

One of my favourites was an outfit to make your own photo, usually a footballer. It consisted of a glass negative, a small packet of sensitised paper, a cardboard frame and two metal clips. The negative was placed in the frame with the sensitised paper behind it, with one clip at the top and one at the bottom to hold it firm. When placed in the sun for a certain length of time it produced a photo on the paper. In my experience, alas, it was always either under- or over-exposed. Nevertheless it was very exciting to produce your own photo of a famous footballer.

My Aunt Carrie – yes, the same Aunt Carrie who as a young girl had had the encounter with Jack the Ripper – lived in Freeman Street, where she sold sweets and drinks made from cordials, hot in the winter, cold in summer. The drinks were sold from a couple of trestle tables placed in the gutter in front of her house. Aunt Carrie had married an Englishman, who not only changed his religion out of love for my aunt, but also changed his name as well to Abraham Abrahams, though I knew him as Uncle Bob. Aunt Carrie was a rather big woman with a strident voice, while Uncle Bob was a mild-mannered man who always seemed to be sitting in their living room whenever I called in to admire Auntie's stock. They had six children, my cousins, Clara, Dungal, Ikey, Yoky, Polly and Julie. They were one of the very few families I knew in the whole of the Tenterground who owned the whole house, all three storeys, and had it all to themselves. Six bedrooms. Luxury!

In Tenter Street, near the alley that led to Bell Lane, was a homemade-toffee shop, with the toffee displayed in tin trays in the window.

The most enterprising of the five sweet shop owners was Debbie Diamond in Shepherd Street near Tilley Street. Whenever the weather permitted it she would raise her bottom window, place a board across from the inside and display her wares to the public. I've an idea she lost one or two items by doing this – so perhaps not a very good idea!

Palacci, the shop we purchased our penn'orth of jam or mustard pickles from, also sold sweets.

CHAPTER NINE

FIRST WEMBLEY FINAL, ITCHY PARK AND PLATZELS, 1923–6

'What are you lot doing here still? Haven't you heard?' I must have been seven years old, when, one day, while playing out in the street with brother Davy and my best friend, Manny Woolf, Morrie Saunders came rushing over to us yelling excitedly. We had no idea what he was talking about but before we had the chance to ask him, he rushed off down the street. So, not wanting to miss any excitement, we dashed off after him.

When we reached Thrawl Street, we could see a large crowd of people on the corner peering up Commercial Street, the main road in the area. 'What's going on?' I shouted at Morrie to make myself heard. 'West Ham are coming,' he replied. I was still completely baffled. 'West Ham are coming?' What on earth did that mean? In the distance we could hear a cheer go up, which got louder and louder as people around us became more and more agitated. Being young and still quite small, we managed to squirm our way through people's legs to get to the front of the crowd. Along the street to our right we could see seven or eight charabancs coming along, all decked out in West Ham Football Club colours with people hanging out the windows, waving to the crowd, holding their scarves out and whirling their rattles.

As one of the coaches went past where we were standing, I suddenly felt a sharp whack on my right ear. Someone had thrown a handful of pennies out of the coach and they'd hit me on the ear. There was a mad scramble all around me to pick up these coins. In spite of my ear stinging badly I managed to hang on to one of the pennies. When the charas had gone by and the crowd dispersed I went across the road to Posner, a large confectioner on the corner of Fashion Street, and purchased one of their famous penny bags. These were already made up and contained toffee, caramels and pieces of chocolate, some small compensation for my aching ear.

The date was 28 April 1923 and the coaches were taking West Ham supporters to the first Cup Final to be played at the new Wembley Stadium. West Ham v. Bolton. I have often wondered since if I was the very first casualty of a Wembley Cup final!

Commercial Street, the street the coaches came down, was our main artery to the great world beyond the Tenterground. It was where we caught the 65 tram to be spirited away. for a modest copper or two, to exotic Bloomsbury or. if you preferred, to Canning Town. The 47 would transport you to Stamford

Hill. This was an especially favourite journey of mine as I could go and visit Mum's friend Ada Bloom and enjoy some of her wonderful tea and cake. She always welcomed me as if I was her own son and never once failed to deliver the goods!

The street started at a big five-pronged junction known as Gardiner's Corner, which took its name from the big store and warehouse on the corner of Commercial Road and Whitechapel High Street. The other members of this junction were Aldgate and Leman Street. It was said that the crossing from Venables, the big ladies' fashion store on the corner of Commercial Street, to Gardiner's was the widest piece of road in London.

It was at Gardiner's Corner that I saw my first fire engine, or, more likely, took any notice of one as I expect I must have seen them before. This happened not long after my encounter with the West Ham supporters. I had gone to Itchy Park with Manny and Morrie when we heard some bells ringing in the distance. Morrie, who seemed to know all these things, said, 'That sounds like a fire engine coming. Quick let's get back to the road.' So we raced out of the park and just as we reached Commercial Street we saw a horse-drawn fire engine tearing along from Gardiner's Corner. It was a magnificent sight, the horses at full gallop and the firemen with their big shiny brass hats on. Hurtling along after them came another large horse-drawn vehicle containing a group of men all wearing big black hats. 'Why aren't those firemen wearing helmets?' I asked. Morrie tutted, 'Don't you know nuffin', Ikey,' he replied, 'They're not firemen, they're the Black 'Ats'. That didn't help very much as I had no idea what a Black Hat was. After tutting some more, Morrie took pity on me and explained that they were the salvage corps who always followed the fire engines to try to save as much property from a burnt-out building as they could.

Although this was the first time I had seen a fire engine careering down the road, it was by no means the last as it became a fairly common sight to see a chimney on fire, with smoke, sparks and even flames pouring out, enveloping the area with acrid fumes and to see the fire brigade turn out to deal with it. Many of these fires could have been prevented by getting the chimney sweep in in time. I suppose the dilemma was a pint, a bet, a packet of fags or the chimney sweep. Perhaps I'm too uncharitable; it could have been between getting something to eat or the sweep, who knows?

If needed, the fire brigade could be summoned from street fire alarms situated on street corners in various strategic locations. They looked like stout red posts about 4-foot 6-inches high with glass set in a frame just below their summit. Around the frame were the words, 'Break Glass, Pull Knob, and wait for the engines.' I'm afraid to say this inscription did occasion some ribald comments from local youngsters.

Itchy Park, where Manny, Morrie and I had been playing before rushing off to see the fire engine, was, in fact, the churchyard of Christ Church and was the only park in the area. It was contained on the outside by a small wall from which sprouted high railings. Along this wall sat the homeless and down-and-outs. It was said the park got its name from these people rubbing their backs against the railings because they were lousy. In between the railings was set a drinking fountain, with a big, heavy metal cup secured by a heavier chain. It was operated by pressing a large metal button, the water emerging from a round hole below it.

Not very large, the park, because it was a churchyard, contained a number of gravestones as well as seats, trees and a few swings. I used to go there with a few friends mainly during the summer, much to the dismay of the more elderly people sitting on the benches hoping to get forty winks. One of my favourite pastimes here was to pick up a few of the numerous caterpillars that seemed to frequent the park. They were mostly little yellow ones, which were found on the barks of the trees. I'd then put them into matchboxes because I had been told that they would eventually grow into butterflies. After watching them carefully for a few days and finding nothing happened I would discard them, box and all.

The entrance to the park was off Commercial Street and stood near to the first block of flats built in the area, dating back to 1864. They were the result of a philanthropic gift from the American, George Peabody, who donated half a million pounds for the 'sole purpose of providing decent housing for London's artisan poor'. Although welcome enough, they were stark cheerless places and whenever I looked at them I felt grateful for my one-floor slum in Palmer Street. One of the things I can remember most about them was that sitting outside the flats along the pavement there was always a row of little old ladies who seemed to eye me with great suspicion as they enjoyed the fresh country air wafting across from the park. I wonder now if some of those old ladies could have been original inhabitants of the flats.

Along the kerb in front of Itchy Park stood a horse trough,

much needed then as most of the traffic serving Spitalfields market was horse-drawn.

Proceeding up Commercial Street from Venables on the right-hand side, there were a number of large buildings, including Commercial Street School, Toynbee Hall, Rothschild's Buildings, Christ Church, Godfrey Phillips cigarette factory and the Cambridge Cinema, before arriving at Shoreditch High Street with Bishopsgate Goods Station on the corner. Going up the left-hand side was the police station, Spitalfields Market, another police station and on to Norton Folgate,

Of all those large buildings there was one that stood out for us young boys. And that was the Cambridge Cinema. Although my visits there partly depended on the state of finances in the Jacobs household, that is to say whether Dad was in work or not, I would go as often as possible because the Cambridge was a Mecca for all us young boys. It stood majestically halfway down Commercial Street, seductively enticing us to enter its noble hall and go along to Saturday Morning Pictures, the meeting place for all the youngsters in the area.

And all it cost was: pit tuppence, circle penny-ha'penny and gallery a penny. I would always try to obtain a penny-ha'penny before going because the circle was the best place to be. It was by no stretch of the imagination the most salubrious of places, being called by those who did not appreciate its finer qualities, the 'Flea Pit', but what did they know?

In those far-off days the films were all silent, words appearing on the screen in place of voices. In the left-hand corner of the stage in front of the screen stood a piano, and on this instrument the pianist would echo the mood of the picture. It was in this very place that many an Indian got his just deserts (as we thought in those unenlightened days). We would be on top of that moving train alongside Buffalo Bill preventing them from boarding it with our accurate fire. How grateful Tom Mix must have felt to us for warning him, often just in the nick of time, of those heathens creeping up behind him. I could quote numerous other instances of how our vigilance prevented the 'red man' from conquering the West, but modesty forbids.

The serial was a more serious business. We had to go and see if Houdini would extricate himself from the deadly peril we left him in at the end of the last episode, chained to the wall by hands and feet with the water rising up to his eyeballs. (Who would be a hero in a serial?) Or maybe we had left Pearl White strapped to that sawbench with the huge circular saw moving ever closer, or bound and gagged across a railway line with the train hurtling along, growing ever closer. (She had a bit of a life too!) To our great relief they would, by some miraculous means, manage to effect their escape at the start of the next episode, only to be back in deeper trouble by its finish, so it was all back next week hoping for another miracle.

The comedies were eagerly awaited by young and old as there was always a comedy with every programme. Ford Sterling and the Keystone Kops, Chester Conklin, Larry Seamon, Harry Langdon, Charlie Chaplin, Buster Keaton, just to name a few of these wonderful comics whose antics kept us schticking in our seats from start to finish.

It was during one of my visits to the Cambridge that I learned of the death of Queen Alexandra, widow of the late King

Edward VII. They flashed it on the screen. Mind you, I don't think it meant that much to me at the time.

The adult pictures were not always well received by the kids unless it was something spectacular. The common or garden love story was tolerated amid much hubbub from the boys waiting to see the programme round again. Programmes were continuous and many a time the porter would come round and ask to see your ticket. If he thought you had been there long enough he'd tell you to get out, and all your protests would fall on deaf ears, – especially if it was Judah Rosenberg in his big peaked hat; I never did like that bloke.

Another cinema I sometimes visited was the Olympia in Shoreditch. Although this didn't normally cater for children I can remember going there once at the age of about ten when they had a special children's afternoon. As well as films they held a series of competitions and so on. I was lucky enough to win a box of dominoes. The spots were various colours and went up to double nine. As soon as I took possession of them I thought to myself, 'I bet Doris will like these.' Although still very young and at the age when I thought all girls were cissies, I did have a soft spot for the girl who lived a few doors down from us and who was about my age, Doris Ruffel. She had long yellow hair, which I found very attractive.

When I got back home I made straight for Doris's house and knocked on her door. When she answered, I said, 'I've got something to show you, Doris.' And I showed her the box of dominoes I'd just won. 'Would you like to come round to my house and play with them?' She nodded and we skipped back along the road. Not knowing how to actually play dominoes, we just matched the numbers all along the floor in my living room. I found I really enjoyed playing with her. It was the first time I had had fun playing with a girl. And for a few days I couldn't get her out of my mind. I didn't really understand my feelings for her as it was nothing I had ever experienced before and it was certainly different to the way I felt about my male friends.

I saw her a couple of times after that out in the street, but although I wanted to see her again and play with her again, I was a bit worried about what my brothers and my friends would say about me playing with a girl. So I took the coward's way out and didn't see her again. Then about a month after this, I saw a lot of people going in and out of her house. One of the people I saw was the doctor with his little black bag. I thought it must be serious if the doctor had been called as generally no one called the doctor unless it was a matter of life or death because hardly anyone in our street could afford one, so no one called one for minor ailments. At first, it wasn't clear what the problem was or who the doctor was seeing, but, after a little while, the doctor left and Mum went round to see what had happened. She was gone for a good half-hour and I was beginning to fear the worst.

When Mum returned, she took me to one side and said, 'Ikey, you were quite sweet on Doris, weren't you?' I blushed a bit. I hadn't realised Mum had known – but then, of course, I should have known that mums know everything. I nodded. 'I'm afraid I have some very bad news. Doris has passed away.' I couldn't believe it. Not Doris! She was only ten years old like me. I felt wretched and it was even worse because I had deliberately stayed away from her over the last couple of weeks through cowardice. I looked down at the ground and suddenly burst into tears. Mum put her arms round me and gave me a big cuddle. Later on that evening I heard Mum tell Dad that Doris had died from blood poisoning. Although, in fact, I didn't really know Doris very well, it took me a long time to recover and I never played with those dominoes again.

I mentioned earlier going down the Lane on a Sunday morning to see Harry Strong knocking out his 'unique' dinner services. But, of course, there was plenty more down the Lane to catch a young boy's imagination. It was the market people flocked to from miles around, especially Jews. The ever-increasing influx of Jews to the area, particularly since the late nineteenth century, had by now stamped the Lane out as a predominantly Jewish market and it always felt to me that it was this Jewish influence that made the Lane what it was and would be for many years to come.

Although the stallholders down the Lane were now principally Jewish, visitors came from all over London and further afield and it was this that was probably responsible for a number of Yiddish words being incorporated into the English language, particularly, but not exclusively, those to do with food. Words such as kosher, beigels, platzels, matzos, schmaltz, lokshen, Shabbos and shul became well-known and fairly commonplace words used by everyone.

Despised by many, tolerated by some and even liked by a few, the Jews and the Lane had become the butt of many music hall jokes, stories, sketches, plays and songs such as 'Abie, Abie, Abie My Boy', 'Yiddle on the Fiddle' and 'Has anyone seen my Yiddisher Boy?' The latter, a plea put to her Victorian and Edwardian audiences by the inimitable Kate Carney, who would go on to tell them that the first time she met him was down the Lane and he was her pride and joy with his 'Oy-yoy-yoy'. All Jews at the time were popularly depicted shaking the palms of their hands up near their ears, chanting 'Oy-yoy-yoy.'

Almost any commodity could be found in its numerous shops and stalls. The best known of its many characters was Fanny Marks, a legend in her own lifetime. She owned a big delicatessen shop which sold many of the little luxuries of life; bucklings, soft, golden cured herrings, red herrings, smoked sprats, anchovies, smoked salmon, pickled herrings, all types of cheeses, olives etc. etc. Fanny Marks never served in the shop; her place was outside on the kerb surrounded by barrels of Dutch herrings. She stood there in all winds and weathers selling only Dutch herrings. She wore big, heavy boots and, in winter, many woollies. People would queue up to be served on Sundays, by far her busiest day. When serving the herrings she would take one out of a barrel, lay it on a cutting board which would lie across another barrel, and with a long, thin, sharp knife cut the head off, gut it, skin both sides, cut it into about a dozen diagonal pieces, pick it up on the knife, lay it on tissue paper and wrap it up in newspaper, the whole operation taking about thirty seconds. Then off she'd go again.

A particular treat at Fanny Marks was when you heard the cry go up, 'The latkes are ready!' These Jewish potato pancakes were originally made as part of the Hanukkah festival but are now available all year round especially the winter. They were cooked freshly on the premises and brought out hot as soon as they were done. There was always a rush when their arrival was announced as they were absolutely delicious and the highlight of any visit down the Lane.

Another fishmonger, Rhuda, apart from selling fish off the slab, also sold live fish from a huge tank in his shop. People would choose the specimen they wanted and he would catch it with a net, behead it and gut it; you couldn't get it much fresher than that! There were quite a few fish stalls in the Lane, the two most renowned being Manny Bogard's and his brother Isaac's, better known to everyone in the area as Darky the Coon, a local villain.

Just across from the Lane in Middlesex Street was Manny Barnet, high-class butcher. He was famed for his salt beef, which could be purchased, ready cooked, by weight or in a sandwich. We bought our sausages and, when in funds, our saveloys, there. They were delicious; never tasted anything like them since we left the area. Opposite Manny Barnet was Blooms, a famous delicatessen.

Baker shops sold various Jewish cakes, bread and rolls, mainly brought over by the more recent influx. Strudel and cheesecake were my favourite types of cake. Various sorts of black and brown bread were sold; I especially enjoyed the bread with caraway seeds in it, but the nicest of all was the *challah* eaten by religious Jews as part of the Sabbath ritual on Friday night. It was an eggy sort of bread shaped like a dozen or so ovals with a separate long bread plait on top running from end to end. We always bought ours from Ostwind's. When in funds and not having to rely on second-rate handouts from Duke Street Shul,

Ostwind was also our baker of choice for Rakusen's or Levy & Levy's matzos to help us celebrate Passover.

The more common or garden everyday rolls took various forms. Beigels, platzels, horseshoes, long rolls and rolls with little seeds on top; all delicious eaten hot and cut open with a bit of Toma margarine.

Dubowsky was famed for his monkey nuts. In the summer, when Mum used to sit outside our front door nattering with the neighbours, I would often be sent there for a pound at a cost of fourpence. They were served hot and straight from the oven in a brown paper bag.

Simon Lewis was the biggest oil shop for a long way round and sold nearly everything that line of business was expected to – it was there I would go to get a pint or two of 'the best nut oil' when Mum was frying. Just before Passover she would fry a big dish of fish, plaice and haddock, for the holiday. The fish would be cut into slices as they were usually big fish, washed and dried and then the frying would commence. As soon as the oil was hot enough the fish would be floured all over, dipped into a large soup plate of well-beaten eggs, ('cracks' usually) and placed in the hot oil. Being a big pan it would take three or four pieces. When the frying was finally over the remaining egg and flour would be beaten together to make delicious pancakes. Yes, when Dad was in work we could eat well enough. Sadly, this was not very often.

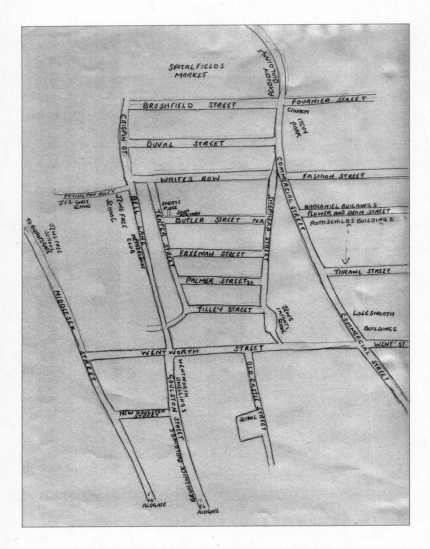

A rough sketch of the Tenterground as I left it in 1925.

CHAPTER TEN

FUMIGATION, BUSSING UP AND EX-LAX, 1926–9

When most of my younger brothers were born, I was really too young to know or understand what was going on. All I knew was that every now and then I'd have a new baby brother to play with, though they took some time getting to the stage where they were old enough to actually play!

It was a bit different with Manny, because I was eight years old when he was born and a bit more aware. I had noticed for some time that Mum seemed to be putting on a lot of weight and even said to her once, 'Mum, why are you getting so fat?' Looking back, probably not the most diplomatic thing I could have said. Dad, who was there at the time, said, 'Don't be so saucy to your mother, Ikey.' So I never did find out!

Then one day, while we were all having our normal slice of bread and marge for lunch, Mum suddenly shouted out, 'It's coming, Jack!' I looked round but couldn't see anything coming and wondered what she was talking about. Dad looked at me and said, 'Ikey, I've got a very important job for you. Run to this address and tell Mrs Grodzinsky that Becky's in labour.' He then gave me a piece of paper with an address in nearby Tilley Street written on it. I felt from the urgency in his voice and from the noises that Mum was making that this could be a matter of life and death, so I rushed off and about fifteen minutes later returned with Mrs Grodzinsky.

In the meantime, Mum had taken to her bed and Julie and all my brothers had been ushered outside to play. 'Good boy, Ikey,' Dad said. 'Now go out and play with your brothers.' I started for the door, then looked back and said, 'Is Mum dying?' I was really worried by all the events of the last half an hour or so. Dad smiled, 'No, of course not,' he reassured me, 'you're going to have another baby brother or sister to play with.' This all seemed very strange to me and I was reluctant to leave, but I did as Dad said, though I couldn't really settle down to playing anything and just sat on the pavement outside wondering what was going on.

After about an hour or so Mrs Grodzinsky, who, I discovered later, was the local midwife, came out of the house and said to me, 'You have another baby brother, Ikey. It was all very quick and easy this time.' This having babies was all a bit mysterious to me and I didn't really know how it was that I had another baby brother, or where he had come from, but, of course, I was quite used to it, as this one was the fifth baby brother to be born. I was glad it was 'all very quick and easy this time' though.

I went back into the house and could hear a baby crying in

Mum and Dad's bedroom, so I looked in the door and saw my Mum holding something in her arms. It was well covered up, so I couldn't see what it was exactly, but I gathered it was the new baby. 'Say hello to Manny,' Dad said. Julie, who had come in with me, burst into tears for some unknown reason. Girls! I thought to myself.

Dad then said he had another special job for me and that was to go to my Aunt Leah (Mum's youngest sister), who lived in faraway Hackney, and tell her that Mum's had the baby. She'll come back with you. He gave me a penny for the tram fare and off I went. Because of the distance I had only visited my Aunt Leah a couple of times, but I liked doing this journey as it was a great adventure for me and, on the couple of occasions I had met Aunt Leah, she had always been very nice to me and usually gave me a few sweets.

Aunt Leah took up residence in our house for a couple of weeks, which did nothing to help our overcrowded situation, but did allow Mum to get a lot of rest, while Leah did all the cooking and cleaning and looking after the rest of us. Though I'm not sure if looking after a screaming baby – and Manny did seem to scream and cry an awful lot – was that much of a rest!

When Aunt Leah left and we were on our own again our overcrowded situation really came home to us. Joey was promoted to our bedroom, which made our sleeping arrangements even more difficult, with four of us having to share the one bed. And, of course, it did absolutely nothing to help alleviate our poverty in the bad times when Dad was out of work – quite the reverse of course.

A few months later, however, help was at hand as the LCC

(London County Council) had decided in its wisdom to demolish most of the Tenterground and build some new flats in their place. We were notified that we would be moved out into a block of flats in Bethnal Green officially called the Boundary Estate, but already known to us simply as Shoreditch Buildings. Though why Shoreditch Buildings I am not quite sure as all the blocks of flats, except for one, were in Bethnal Green. Just Cleeve Buildings was in Shoreditch. This estate had been built several years earlier as part of another slum clearance plan when the notorious area known as the Nichol was demolished. The Nichol's claim to fame had been that it was thought to house the highest proportion of villains per head of population in London.

It might be worth just recapping a brief history of the Nichol here, an area made famous by Arthur Morrison in his book, *A Child of the Jago*, published in 1896 – the Jago being a fictionalised name for the Nichol, a warren of very densely populated streets, alleys and courts. It was said that some 6000 people lived within this small neighbourhood and it was avoided like the plague by people from outside the area because of its evil reputation as a low slum district populated in the main by villains and criminals. It was a thorn in the side of the local authorities and the police for many years and it was decided that the only way to deal with the problem was to demolish the whole lot and replace it with some model buildings, the very same Boundary Estate we were now moving to.

Its name, the Nichol, came from the fact that four of the main roads in the area had Nichol in their name. There was

Nichol Street, Half Nichol Street, New Nichol Street and the only one which still survives, Old Nichol Street.

The blocks of flats on the Boundary Estate were spread out around a central circular park area known as Arnold Circus with each block being named after a village on the Thames. I suppose they thought if they named places like Chertsey or Cookham it would make people think they were living in idyllic surroundings. So, towards the end of 1925 we said farewell to our second floor flat in Palmer Street and moved off to 22 Sunbury Buildings.

Before we were allowed to move in however, the council took all our bedding and other articles that might harbour bugs and fumigated them. It was a strict council rule that this had to be done for all people moving from slum areas, for which, I might say, the Tenterground nobly qualified.

"Ere this is a bit of all right, eh Jack?' said Mum after we'd had a chance for a quick look round our new home. 'Three bedrooms. Never was such times.'

Meanwhile us kids were all excitedly rushing around the rooms and outside on the landing seeing what else we could find in our new surroundings. As we were scampering around, Davy suddenly gave a squawk and shouted, 'Look!' We looked. He had opened the door at the end of the landing and had found a toilet. 'No more shitting in the cold and dark,' he trumpeted and jumped up and down with delight. Then Bill saw a big sink with two taps, 'No more 'aving to fetch water up the apples.' This was all truly luxurious.

As we were running up and down whooping and screaming our delight, one of the doors on the landing opened (there were five flats per landing altogether). A rather large rotund woman with jet black hair peered out, 'What's going on?' she yelled. 'What's all this bloody noise about?' We stopped suddenly. As the eldest boy, it was down to me to explain and make peace with the woman. 'Please, miss,' I began hesitantly, 'we're sorry.'

'Are you the new family?' she asked.

'I suppose we are,' I replied.

'Well, OK, I'll forgive you this once, but if you ever make a bloody row like that again, I'll have you thrown out the buildings.'

That was our first meeting with Rachel Freeman. She and her family, consisting of husband Nat and six children, held a rather privileged position on our floor. Their flat was bigger than everyone else's and actually had a self-contained toilet and sink inside the flat. We learned it didn't do to cross them.

Wanting to get away from Mrs Freeman, we decided to go downstairs and see what was down there. In Palmer Street we had been used to going straight out into the road, but here in Sunbury Buildings, downstairs led to a large enclosed area, which was officially called the yard, but we were later to come to know it as our playground. Though our idea of it being a playground led to us into all sorts of trouble over the years.

On our very first morning we ran into Mr Shaw, though, of course, we didn't know his name then. As we came hurtling down the stairs and out into the yard, we could see a man sweeping up over on the other side. We didn't really take any notice and started kicking stones around. He came rushing over, shouting at us. 'Oi, whaddya fink yer doin'?' Again it fell to me to be our spokesman. 'Playing,' I said. 'Not in my yard, yer not,' he replied. 'This yard is not for 'ooligans like you to rush around disturbin' everyone.' I looked around but couldn't see anyone. 'There's no one here to disturb,' I said by way of a reasonable comment. 'I'm 'ere!' came the equally reasonable reply. 'Now piss off out of 'ere, the lot of you.'

So, thrown off the landing for making a noise, thrown out the yard for playing, I was beginning to wish we'd never moved from Palmer Street, even if we didn't have to shit in the cold and dark any more! No one worried about running around and making a noise in the Tenterground. This all seemed a bit too posh for the likes of us and that night, once the initial excitement of moving had worn off, I became engulfed in sadness at the thought of leaving such a paradise as 20 Palmer Street. All right, so it was a bit buggy, lousy and dilapidated, but that didn't stop it from being a Heaven on Earth to the child it had lovingly nurtured for seven years. Perhaps to its parents it did, but then they didn't see things in their right perspective. I'm not too ashamed to admit I cried myself to sleep that night but there was nothing I could do about the situation as a new chapter in our lives inevitably and inexorably opened up before us.

For some time after our move, I continued to return to the dingy cobbled streets I loved so well, even though most of it had been redeveloped, just to soak up what atmosphere was left. Aunt Carrie moved into a block of flats known as Brune House, one of the buildings built where my beloved Tenterground had once been. Visiting her one day, I was aghast when I heard her say to Mum, 'My life, Becky, I can't tell you how much I enjoy living here, it's so much better than that slum of a house we had in Freeman Street.' To me, this smacked of outright treachery. I felt it was that kind of talk that had lost us our true heritage of rows and rows of terraced back-to-back slums!

The following day, we ventured out again but not long after we got to the playground I heard someone shouting, 'Oi, you, what's yer name?' I looked round and saw three boys coming out from the bottom of the stairwell. I didn't answer. 'Oi, I'm talkin' to you,' said the biggest of the three boys. He looked about my age but must have been an inch or so taller than me. He walked towards us and, not wanting any trouble, I replied, 'I'm Ikey.'

'What you doin' in 'ere, Ikey?' he asked, still coming towards us. 'This is only for us what live 'ere. Clear off back to the street.'

'We do live here,' I protested, 'we've just moved into number 22.'

For some reason, when I said this, Joey ran up to the boy and said, 'D'you wanna make somefin' of it?' I pulled Joey off but I could see the three boys bristling and my brothers lining up behind me and Joey getting ready for a fight.

One of the other boys looked at Joey and laughed. "E's a bit of a tearaway, ain't 'e?' For some reason this seemed to break the atmosphere and the lead boy said, 'OK, OK, no trouble. Just wanted to make sure you lived 'ere. All Sunburyites welcome 'ere.'

It didn't seem likely at the time but that spokesman for the three boys was soon to become my new best friend. His name was Hymie Marcovitch and he liked playing all the games I liked such as glarnies (our name for marbles) and ciggies. In fact, like me, he was an avid cigarette card collector and many's the time we went off to Liverpool Street Station in search of these oblong pieces of card. We would pester the people getting on and off their trains when we saw them opening up their cigarette packets, ''Ere mister, can I have your fag card please?' Most would give them, a few would swear at us and tell us to 'piss off' or worse, but it was worth it as we usually came back with a goodly haul from a couple of hours at the station.

I enjoyed my visits to Liverpool Street Station for another reason and that was seeing all the steam engines blowing their hooters and belching smoke and grit into the already heavily polluted atmosphere. It was a magnificent sight and I dreamt about the places these trains would be going, exotic places like Chingford or Epping, some even to the seaside to places we knew were far beyond our reach and would never be able to get to like Southend and Clacton.

In addition, right opposite the station stood Bishopsgate Fire Station. As soon as we heard the fire bells ring we would race out of the station to see those brave men set out to put out fires and rescue those trapped in some raging inferno or other.

It took a while to fall into the ways of the Buildings. We discovered that Mr Shaw was one of three 'Guardians of the Yard' whose job it was to sweep up every day and otherwise keep it clean and tidy. The other two were Mr Eaton and Mr Ashford. Their boss was Mr Foot, who had the grand title of Superintendent. We also learnt that the three guardians had very set times when they would come and sweep up, so that for the rest of the day, the yard could become our playground with no one there to stop us. Occasionally, Mr Foot put in an unexpected visit and, if he found us larking about, would threaten to tell our parents. I don't know whether he did or not, but nothing was ever said to us by Mum and Dad.

It didn't take us long to find out that because everyone knew the times of the three Guardians hardly anyone took any notice of the restriction not to play in the yard as, after school, the playground became a hive of activity as the children from the buildings took up all available space with their games. The girls skipping and playing ball, the boys mostly playing football or cricket. Leapfrog and diabolo were still popular, but I was introduced to two new games I hadn't encountered in the Tenterground. The first was called pick-a-back fighting and involved two boys, each having a smaller boy riding pick-a-back on his shoulders, whose job it was to try and pull his opponent off. The two larger boys would circle each other to try and find a good opening for their jockey. Naturally, the one who pulled the other's rider off was proclaimed the winner.

The other game was 'bussing up', this involved two boys standing side by side and linking up by placing their inside arms around the other's back. They would then run up and down the playground like a pair of lunatics, scattering all in their path.

A common practice at the time, especially for those kids living on the top floor, was to call up to your mother to throw down a slice of bread and butter. This would come hurtling down a little later wrapped in newspaper and announce its arrival with a small thump on the ground.

Naturally with slightly more violent games than we were used to there seemed to be a lot more friction around, with accidents, fights and name calling and mothers having to intervene. My mum was often at the centre of these altercations as me and my brothers tended to stick together, becoming known as the Jacobs Gang with an injury to one an injury to all. One occasion I remember was when Davy got knocked over by two boys, Mossy Abrahams and Jack Cohen, who were flying around the playground in their bus-up. I saw what had happened and went over to confront them, followed by my other brothers.

'Oi, Mossy,' I shouted, 'look what you've done to Davy.'

''E'll be all right,' replied Mossy; 'tell 'im to get up.'

'Say sorry to 'im,' I said.

'Don't be so wet,' put in Jack. ''E got in our way, it wasn't our fault, 'e should've looked where 'e was going.'

At this, Bill, who must have been a couple of years younger than Jack Cohen, just went over to him and biffed him in the moosh. Jack got hold of him and was just about to hit him back when I intervened and a free-for-all started with the Jacobs Gang and our allies taking on Mossy and Jack's friends. As it happened, Jack's nose had started bleeding where Bill had hit him and he went running back home. Minutes later, unbeknown to me, Jack's mum was round at our flat, pounding on the door. When Mum opened it, Mrs Cohen pointed at her Jack's nose and said, 'Look what one of your boys 'as done.'

'What d'you mean, one of my boys? My boys wouldn't do a thing like that,' replied Mum.

'Oh, wouldn't they? Tell 'e, Jack.'

So Jack told her how Bill had hit him. But Mum would have none of it. 'My boys are too well brought up to do a thing like that,' she said, and then, somewhat contradictorily, added, 'and even if 'e did, I expect you deserved it.'

''Ow dare you, you *yente*,' replied Mrs Cohen. 'My boy did nuffin'. Your Bill just attacked 'im for no reason and broke 'is nose. It won't never be right again.'

'Oh piss off, Rachel, and take your lying son of a bitch with you. Bill, of all people, 'e wouldn't 'urt a fly.'

'My son's not a liar, if 'e said it 'appened it 'appened,' said Mrs Cohen indignantly.

But Mum was in no mood to take this lying down, 'Look, we all know what a lying bastard your Jack is,' she said.

'And we all know what a set of fuckin' little thugs you've brought up, Becky,' replied Mrs Cohen.

''Ow dare you! Don't you swear at me, you fuckin' *nafka*,' warned Mum, 'or, on my life, you can kiss my *tuches*.'

By this time Jack had run off back to the playground and it looked for all the world as if there was going to be another fight, only this time on the third floor of Sunbury Buildings between two otherwise respectable mothers. However, after a few more slanderous allegations and insinuations were bandied about, particularly about whether the other's child was born in wedlock, Mrs Cohen and Mum decided that honour had been satisfied in standing up for their own respective whiter-than-white child and the slanging match finished as Mrs Cohen returned to her flat.

Now, the funny thing was that by the time this fracas upstairs was over, the fighting had stopped and we were all happily playing football together, Bill and Jack included, ill-feelings forgotten as though nothing had happened and completely

Above left: Alfie's parents, Jack – formally known as John – and Rebecca, in the mid to late 1930s. They were introduced to each other by Sarah, Jack's younger sister.

Above right: Alfie – formally known as Isaac – in 1938, aged twenty-three. This photo was taken a year before he enlisted in the army for the Second World War. The photo is inscribed 'to Joyce, with love, Alf'.

Below right: Joyce Sinnott, Alfie's sweetheart, *c.*1940, aged twenty. She and Alfie met through their mutual friend, Teddy, in the late 1930s.

Left: On the left is the Jews' Free School; the entrances to the school were located on Middlesex Street, Strype Street and Bell Lane. Both Jack and Alfie attended the school, from the ages of seven to thirteen.

Right: An illustration by Robert Barltrop of the Soup Kitchen for the Jewish Poor, located on Butler Street – in the heart of the Tenterground. The Soup Kitchen became essential for providing the Jacobs family with food in the years following the First World War.

Left: Marlow Buildings which, like Sonning Buildings and Sunbury Buildings, formed a part of the Boundary Estate housing development, located on the cusp of Bethnal Green and Shoreditch. In the late 1930s, the council relocated the Jacobs family from Sonning Buildings to Marlow Buildings.

Left: Joe Assenheim's ice-cream barrow, located on Petticoat Lane. The ice cream was sold, as Alfie recalls, 'in oblong shapes wrapped in plain white paper, half strawberry and half cream'.

Right: The Cleeve Workshops – also a part of the Boundary Estate – where Alfie began his first job, as a milkman, in 1927, and retired from his career as a woodcarver in 1981. This door, to no. 1 Cleeve Workshops, housed the woodcarving workshop that Alfie worked in.

Left: The Battle of Cable Street, on Sunday, 4 October 1936, between Sir Oswald Mosley's Blackshirts and members of the East London Jewish community, the Labour Party and the Communist Party.

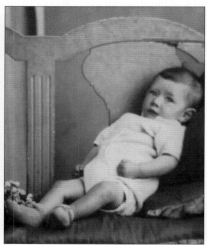

Above left: Alfie in 1959, aged forty-three, working in his woodcarving workshop. After finishing his woodcarving apprenticeship in the early 1930s, he earned 1/6d per hour which, after a few years, increased to 2 shillings per hour.

Above right: Alfie in 1940, aged twenty-four, when he enlisted in the army for the Second World War. He was promised that his job as a woodcarver would be kept safe for his return.

Below left: Alfie and Joyce in about 1940 – with Alfie in his military uniform.

Below right: The first child of Alfie and Joyce, born in 1940, five months before Alfie was called to the army for the Second World War. By Jewish tradition, their child was named after Alfie's father, John.

oblivious to what was going on between our mums. But this little scenario, or something like it, was a regular occurrence in the Buildings as might be expected when a large number of children are playing in the same restricted space.

Although these fights did break out occasionally, we mostly got on with each other, though that's not to say we didn't play tricks on one another. One day, a boy called Morrie White, who was a friend of Davy's, came to our flat to play. For the life of me I can't remember why, but, for some reason we had a lot of small samples of Ex-lax (a chocolate laxative) in the flat. In appearance they looked like small bars of chocolate Neapolitans. Davy and I plied him with quite a few of these as he seemed to be enjoying them and even said to us, 'I like these ex-chocolates, where do you get them?' 'Oh, from the sweet shop,' Davy replied casually.

The next day, his mother came knocking on our day and demanded to know from Mum what her Morrie had been eating the day before. Mum, who knew nothing of what we had done, shrugged her shoulders and said, 'What do you mean, Esther? 'E just had a couple of sweets, I think. Why d'you ask already?' 'Cos,' replied Esther, 'mein Morrie's been running in and out o' the *dreck* 'ouse all night.' 'Well it was nothin' 'e 'ad 'ere,' said Mum concluding the interview and shutting the door.

Something else we had to get used to in the Buildings was the fact that we were supposed to help keep the place clean. In the Tenterground we just had our own little living space to worry about, but here there was much more sense of communal living. Under the single gaslight that faced the stairs on each landing was a notice written in English and Hebrew stating that the stairs and landing had to be cleaned once a week by the five tenants in rotation. The penalty for failing to carry out this duty was notice to quit. Under the notice, the flat number of that week's cleaner was placed in a frame.

Notice to quit was also the penalty for failing to pay the weekly rent on time. The rent had to be paid into the Estate Office in Calvert Avenue every Monday morning before twelve noon. A minute late and it would not be accepted and notice to quit given. The chief clerk, to whom the rent was paid, was a Mr Richardson, but was universally known to everyone as the 'Black Bastard'. It was always the woman's job to pay the rent and they swore that Mr Richardson was so strict and delighted in giving notice to quit because he had once been crossed in love and was out for revenge on all women.

In the evenings, it was the duty of the porters to light the landing lights. More often than not they delegated this task to one of us boys as they didn't fancy the walk up and down the stairs. The first time I got delegated was not long after we moved in. I was downstairs playing near the entrance one evening when one of the porters called to me, 'Oi you, 'ow'd yer like to earn a joey?' (A joey was what we called a silver threepenny piece.) 'Yes sir, I'd love to,' I replied. 'Well, if you turn the lights on and if I fink you's done a good job, I'll give you the thruppence.' He gave me some long tapers and a box of matches and told me to get on with it. The gas had to be turned on from a downstairs cupboard, then I had to light the taper and race up and down the stairs in our block lighting the lamps.

When I returned I gave him back the tapers and matches I had left over and held out my hand for my reward. 'You took too long,' he said, 'you don't get nuffin' for that.' And he walked off. I later learnt from the other boys that he never in fact paid any of us any money, but that didn't stop us volunteering to do the job as it was good fun running up and down the stairs, lighting the lamps.

This didn't last for long though, as electricity was soon introduced into the Buildings, replacing gas as the main form of lighting both in the flats and on the stairs and landings. While they were digging out the channels in the playground to lay the cables, Joey stumbled into one of them and broke his arm.

A month or so after we moved in, we had another encounter with Mrs Freeman on our landing. Mum was trying to get Manny to walk and sometimes walked along the landing with him, with her holding one hand and Julie holding the other.

One day they were doing this when Mrs Freeman suddenly appeared at her door brandishing a knife. She then walked up behind Mum, Julie and Manny and waved the knife up and down between Manny's legs. 'What the bloody hell are you doing?' asked Mum, quite reasonably given the circumstances. Mrs Freeman replied, 'I'm cutting the string that's holding his legs together. Now he'll walk.'

Mum hurriedly took Manny and Julie back indoors and said to Dad, 'That woman next door's doolally.' This incident only reinforced Mum's opinion of Mrs Freeman though. Because although she was 'Queen of the landing' by virtue of having a bigger flat than everyone else, she was also one of those fairly recent immigrants from Eastern Europe that Mum dismissed as Pullocks.

A few days after this, we heard a big commotion coming from the next-door flat where Mr and Mrs Lyons lived. There was some banging and crashing and then screaming. The walls were not that thick and we could hear Mr Lyons yelling at his wife, 'Don't you fuckin' tell me what to do, you fuckin' *nafka*!' There was then a loud thump as though someone had fallen over on to the table or something. Then we heard Mrs Lyons scream, 'Solly, please!' and Mr Lyons reply, '*Ikh hob dir in drerd*!' (which even with our limited knowledge of Yiddish knew meant something like, 'Go to Hell!') and then another thump.

The sound coming from next door was loud enough to wake up the whole landing and suddenly we heard the door from next door the other way fly open and we looked out to see our neighbours on the other side, Mr and Mrs Perrin, rush round to the Lyonses'. 'Fuck off, Natie,' Mr Lyons bellowed, 'this is none of your business.' 'Solly, Solly, calm down,' said Mr Perrin soothingly. 'I'm sure we can talk this through.' 'I've warned you, Natie, just fuck off and leave us alone.' Meanwhile Mrs Perrin was talking to Mrs Lyons: 'Has he hurt you again, Hannah?' All she got by way of reply as far as we could hear was loud sobbing. 'Come with me, Hannah, let's go back to our place.' Then Mr Lyons in a very threatening voice, 'Fuck off both of you. She doesn't want to go back to your place you interfering *alte kaker*. She's my fuckin' wife and we'll settle this ourselves.'

The two men continued to talk while Mrs Perrin continued to comfort Mrs Lyons. Gradually Mr Lyons began to calm down and about an hour after it had all started Mr and Mrs Perrin went back to their flat, leaving the Lyons on their own.

But we heard nothing more from them that night. The next day we saw Mrs Lyons leave her flat and we noticed she had a black eye and a few cuts on her face.

This occurrence happened several more times over the next year and each time the Perrins came round to calm Mr Lyons down and care for Mrs Lyons. We later learnt that Mr Lyons was, in fact, a very sick man himself and suffered from a nervous disorder brought on, it was said, by his experience in the trenches during the First World War and this is what led to him taking it out on his wife. In those days these sorts of incidents were viewed very differently to today. There was no such place as a women's shelter where battered wives could go and the police were very reluctant to get involved in what they saw as a purely domestic issue. There was also very little recognition of the stress brought on by serving in the trenches, what we might call post-traumatic stress disorder these days.

Oddly enough, Mrs Lyons's saviours, the Perrins, also suffered from domestic problems. Mr Perrin was an alcoholic and would come home at all hours of the day and night shouting and throwing things around, though he was never actually violent towards his wife. The fact that he worked in a brewery probably didn't help matters though.

Gracie Perrins and Hannah Lyons were sisters and had moved into the Buildings with their respective husbands a couple of years before we did. About a year after we moved in, both families moved out and we had to get used to new neighbours, who, fortunately made less noise and lived much quieter lives.

Into the Lyonses' flat came Harry Gordon and his wife

'Fuffer'. This was the only name anyone ever called her. I can't believe it was her real name though. Harry was a decent sort and became a new source of revenue for me as he would often ask me to go to the shop for him and get him a packet of fags. He never failed to cough up at least a penny for running this errand for him.

Fuffer was a bit peculiar and had this habit of sidling up to you and speaking in to your ear in a very hushed whisper as though telling you some great secret that mustn't be overheard at all costs. One day she came into our house and whispered into Mum's ear that our local fishmonger, Johnny Hughes, had some 'very nice haddockskis and codskis'. This became a standing joke in our family for years and whenever she bought one of these fish, Mum would say, 'We've got haddockski [or codski] for tea tonight.'

Our new neighbours the other side was a family we already knew well from the Tenterground as they had lived in Shepherd Street. None other than the Da Costas, Mick and Annie, with the two boys, Jackie and Aaron, whom I also knew from the Jews' Free School. The elder, Jackie, was not Mick's son. He was the result of a wartime romance that had left Annie literally holding the baby. Whether the father was killed or had just waltzed off we never knew.

Mick was known to us as Mickey Flat, a name Mum gave him because of his flat nose. He had no real profession and just did odd jobs in Spitalfields Market to earn money. This wasn't a great source of income and Annie used to complain to Mum that Mickey only gave her 'firty-free shillings a week'.

One of the first jobs he undertook on moving in next door

was to lay some new lino, so he got Annie to take the two boys out while he attended to this time-consuming but, as he thought, ultimately rewarding chore and essential house improvement. For hour after hour all we could hear was the noise of banging coming from his flat. Eventually the noise stopped and we heard a knock at the door. It was Mick, who invited us all in to look at his handiwork. There, under the table, was an oblong piece of lino, about six foot by three, held down by hundreds of tacks, almost to the point of making a metal border. Mick stood there beaming, waiting for our praise and approbation to be heaped upon him. I don't think the noise coming out of that flat was praise when Annie got back!

The other flat on our landing housed a war widow, Mrs Hollander. She also left shortly after our arrival. Nothing to do with us I don't think. She remarried and went to live in her new husband's house.

Into her place came Wally Betts, his wife and two children, both boys. Wally had been gassed during the war and was a very sick man. He could barely get around and his movements were painfully slow. Mrs Betts used to go out to work to earn money for the family, leaving poor Wally stuck on his own at home most days.

One evening at about six o'clock, we heard her door open and shut as she returned home and shortly afterwards a piercing scream. We opened our door to see what had happened and we saw Mrs Betts rush out of her flat yelling, 'Help! Help! Somebody help me!' We were not alone in opening our door as everyone on the landing was soon outside trying to find out what had happened. 'What is it?' Mum said to her. 'It's Wally,' she sobbed. 'He's drunk a bottle of Lysol.' Fuffer sidled over to Mum's side and whispered in her ear, 'Lysol. Hopeless.' And so it was. Poor Wally was dead. Suicide. Yet another victim, along with the Lyonses, Mrs Hollander and Annie Da Costa, of the war to end all wars.

CHAPTER ELEVEN

FIZZY DRINKS, POETRY AND EMPIRE DAY, 1926–9

Our move to new surroundings with three bedrooms and indoor toilet and sink, though welcome in one way, did nothing to help alleviate our poverty and we were still very much dependent on charity most of the time. Two adults and seven growing children would have taxed even the pocket of a man in full time employment, but Dad was still out of work more than he was in it. So we still needed all the help we could get.

The Soup Kitchen was much further away now and it took two of us to carry our food back, one to carry the groceries, bread and so on in a pillow case, the other to carry the soup can, which was placed in a market bag and carried holding both the handles of the can and the bag. This task usually fell to Davy and me as the two oldest boys. Whereas the Soup Kitchen had only been a couple of streets away in the Tenterground, we now had to negotiate a much longer journey, with no little apprehension I can tell you, along dark and dismal dosser-strewn pavements.

On the plus side though we now passed a yard in Wheeler Street where we sometimes paused to look at the Foden steam wagons it housed and, even better, if we were lucky, sometimes saw them returning to base. What a sight they were with smoke belching from their funnels and red-hot ashes falling into a large tray between the front wheels as they chugged along Commercial Street.

We still relied heavily on BMC tickets and found a new source of supply nearer to our new home in Mr Brody of the Jewish Boys' Club in Chance Street, just the other side of Old Nichol Street.

We continued to visit the Board of Guardians and the Bun House as well as Ada Bloom up in Stamford Hill. Here we were fortunate in having two trams and a bus much closer to our new home than in Palmer Street. At Passover we still got our matzos from Booth Street Shul.

The main recipient of our BMC tickets was now Woolfy Rees, who owned a small grocer shop nearby, which he ran with his wife. They had two children, Sylvie and Mickey, round about my age. Woolfy was as bald as a coot with not a single hair on his head.

In the summer Woolfy Rees's shop was well-known for its cold drinks. He had a big glass contraption by an open window bearing the name Vantas on it. This machine had a large handle at the side. Once you had handed over your ha'penny for a glass of lemonade or cream soda or whatever you fancied, Woolfy would pour some syrup from a large bottle into a glass and then hold the glass under the machine. He would then pull the large handle and a mighty hissing and bubbling would ensue till the glass was filled with aerated water, which combined with the syrup to make a delicious fizzy drink. It would have been worth paying the ha'penny just to see and hear the contraption working even if the drink hadn't been very refreshing.

Fortunately not everything relied on us having to pay money for it and we, along with all the other residents in the Buildings, were able to enjoy ourselves in the Bandstand without worrying about the cost.

The Bandstand at the centre of the Buildings was the chief meeting place mainly for the elderly, especially in the summer when all the seats – and there were a lot of them – would be occupied. The Bandstand was built on two levels. There was a flight of stairs up from the street to a concrete circle where many of the seats were situated. Between the street, Arnold Circus, and this first level there were numerous flower beds encircling the whole area. These were maintained by the local council and were always in full bloom, looking very attractive. From this level there were more steps leading up to the Bandstand itself, around which more seats were placed. When two friends met up, the conversation usually started with, '*A gutn tog! Vi geyt es?*'

'*Es geyt gut, a dank! Un dir?*'

'*Nishkoshe.*'

'*Vos iz es faran neyes?*'

'*Nit fil.*'

Or some such and it would go on from there. Anyone who

spoke only English would be completely out of their depth trying to understand what the old folks were talking about as the mother tongue of the Bandstand was most definitely Yiddish.

The Bandstand would be even more packed on Tuesday evenings during the summer as this was when brass bands gave a two-hour concert of popular music. As well as those sitting round the Bandstand, all the windows in the buildings around Arnold Circus and its side streets would be pushed up from the bottom giving the inhabitants a view of the band as well as allowing the notes to reach right into their front rooms. While the performance went on, fruit, nuts and various sweetmeats would be handed round and consumed in vast quantities and a general air of gaiety prevailed. The programme mostly consisted of a selection of popular songs which the audience often joined in by singing the words.

We children used to play around the Bandstand all the time as well and we didn't stop for the music. If we got too noisy though we'd be told in no uncertain terms to 'bugger off!'

The favourite piece, which was played every week, was 'The Post Horn Gallop'. The soloist would stand up and a great hush descend over the whole Bandstand and surrounding area. He would then pick up a long thin post horn, the type used in the heyday of the stagecoach of yesteryear, and put his heart and soul into his rendition, which was always met with thunderous applause that echoed all round the Buildings.

The concert lasted from 7:00 p.m. to 9:00 p.m., when 'The King' (that is, 'God Save the King') brought the evening to a happy and successful close. The audience then dispersed to their homes and we kids would go to bed.

The Bandstand was mainly used for another purpose during the daytime as it was said to be a mile round, though obviously it was nothing like that. But it enabled us to hold quarter-, half- and one-mile races. Older boys would sometimes hold 'marathons' of an agreed number of laps. But these always ended in an argument as the loser would invariably accuse the winner of not completing the requisite number.

Because we had moved house it was also now more convenient for me to change schools and attend Virginia Road School, just a minute's walk away from the Buildings. Mum told me that I had to report to the Headmaster, Mr McInnes, as soon as I arrived on my first day, which I dutifully did. He was a tall Scotsman with a round, very red face.

'Good morning, Ikey,' he said, with very little trace of a Scottish accent. 'Good morning, sir,' I mumbled. He then proceeded to tell me a bit about the school and what was expected of me, I think. I say I think because I wasn't really listening to him as I was fascinated by a large framed print hanging on the wall behind him. It was of the famous *Punch* illustration showing the German Kaiser and the King of Belgium with the caption, Kaiser: 'So, you have lost everything.' King of the Belgians: 'Not my soul.' At the time I had no idea what this was about but I knew the Kaiser was a baddie because we kids used to sing a song that went,

'The Kaiser sat in a box of eggs, parley-voo.
The Kaiser sat in a box of eggs, parley-voo
The Kaiser sat in a box of eggs
And all the yellow ran down his legs,
Inky pinky parley-voo.'

As well as this defiant cartoon in his office, the headmaster had also hung a plaque in the hall inside a large mahogany frame, with the school motto, taken from Sir Henry Newbolt's poem 'Vitaï Lampada', 'Play up! play up! and play the game!' Virginia Road was a very proud school that wanted to instil a sense of fairness and honour amongst its pupils. I like to think it worked on me.

My new school only had five classes and five masters and teachers along with the head. My class master was Mr Wiggins, who also taught history to the whole school.

One of the other teachers was a Miss Dix, for some reason known to us all as Aunt Sally. One morning, about a year after I started, Mr McInnes called us all into the main hall and said, 'Boys and girls I have some very sad news to tell you, and that is that Miss Dix died yesterday.' Some of the girls began crying and this tragic news did come as a big shock to all of us as, firstly, she was very popular and a well-loved teacher, and, secondly. she seemed quite young. The story quickly went round the school that she had set light to herself by smoking in bed. Whether this was true or not I was never sure.

Her place was taken by Mr Barnett, who strangely enough, given that the pupils at the school were overwhelmingly Jewish, was the first Jewish master to be employed there. I already knew about Mr Barnett as he had been a teacher at a nearby school, Rochelle Street School. The reason I already knew of him was because my friend, Hymie Marcovitch, went to Rochelle Street and he had told me all about him, about how strict he was and it didn't do to get on the wrong side of him. In fact, he painted him out to be a bit of a tyrant. But my impression of him was completely the opposite. I found him to be very kind with a really good sense of humour. Of course, if you did disobey him or play up in his class he wouldn't be so kind, but that was only to be expected.

Generally I liked school and enjoyed most lessons. I especially liked poetry, and I learned a number of classic poems off by heart. My favourites were 'The Private of the Buffs' by Sir Francis Hastings Doyle, which supposedly told the heroic story of Private John Moyse, captured by the Chinese during the Second Opium War but who refused to bow to them and was summarily executed, and 'Vitaï Lampada', the poem from which the school's motto came. I can still remember them to this day.

My least favourite lessons were singing and art. Mr Rush was our singing teacher and he would play the piano while we sang all the standard songs such as 'Barbara Allen', 'Golden Slumbers' and 'Sweet and Low'. One day, whilst in full flow, Mr Rush suddenly stopped playing and held his hand up. 'Stop,' he commanded, 'I am going to ask some of you to come out here and sing solos.' We all looked at each other a bit apprehensively. Over the next few minutes he called out a few individuals and asked them to sing a few bars. All went well as Mr Rush usually muttered something like, 'Good, good,' before dismissing the boy back to his seat. Then his eyes lighted on me. 'You, Ikey Jacobs, you're next.' I went out to the front a bit nervous, but I managed a few bars of 'Barbara Allen' before Mr Rush held up his hand and said, 'Stop! Please return to your seat and never sing in my class again.' So I never did. Was I really that bad? I think I know what my wife and children will say to that when they see this little story!

Apart from all the old standards, one other song we sang – well, the rest of the class sang and I listened to – was 'When I was a Lad' from *H.M.S. Pinafore*. This further whetted my appetite for Gilbert and Sullivan. I had read about them and their operas on cigarette cards and now I had actually heard one of their songs, which I really liked. I definitely felt now that I wanted to find out more about them and go and see one of the operas if I could, but, of course, such a thing was completely out of the question. We never had that sort of money.

I never could get to grips with art. We were told how to make pictures appear three dimensional, all about plans and elevations and so on, but it was all like a foreign language to me. I wasn't too good at the offshoots either. We had metalwork once a week and the only thing I can remember making was a copper ash tray which stayed in our family for many years, though I never used it personally as I never took up smoking. The only interest I had in smoking was the cigarette cards that came in the packets.

Woodwork classes were held in a nearby school whose name escapes me. I made a number of items, such as a pencil sharpener, a square block of wood with a piece of sandpaper stuck on to it; a teapot stand and other items just as useless.

The highlights of my time at school were when we were taken out on visits. For example, we were once taken to Cambridge Heath Gas Works to learn how gas was made and stored. An official of the Gaslight and Coke Company showed us round. It was exciting seeing the retorts where the coal was heated and turned into gas. He also told us how the by-products were made and marketed and how the residue of the coal, coke, was sold to industry and the public.

Another visit we made was to Cadby Hall in Hammersmith, the home of Lyons Tea, to see how tea was sorted and packaged.

One morning in assembly, Mr McInnes announced we were very honoured to have an important guest. It was none other than our local MP, Percy Harris. He told us that Mr Harris would be coming round during the day to visit each class and we all had to be on our best behaviour. When he reached our class, we all stood as he strode to the front of the class. 'Sit down, sit down,' he said and then told us that 'School days are the happiest days of your life. Once you get out into the big world you will find things difficult; some of you will get on, others won't. The important thing to remember is that the more you learn at school, the more likely you are to get a better job.' He then asked us if we had any problems, were we happy at school, were we happy at home and so on. Finally he said he was going to ask us some general knowledge questions to see how much we had learnt at school. One of these was 'What do we call those little birds that fly about our streets all day?' While I was pondering this, Simon Davis shot his hand up into the air. 'Yes, you,' said Mr Harris. 'They're called dicky birds, sir,' replied a very pleased-with-himself Simon.

At the end of the day, Mr Harris invited a number of us along to meet him at the House of Commons. I was one of the lucky few chosen and on the appointed day we met him outside Parliament and he showed us round, telling us about its workings and traditions. The only thing I remembered of this guided tour was that for some reason a man called Black Rod knocks on a door three times.

Percy Harris was the MP for South West Bethnal Green for over twenty years from 1922 to 1945. A Jew, he was the only Liberal MP for miles around. He worked tirelessly for the underdog. During the depression of the 1930s, he opened up the Bethnal Green Men's Institute to keep men off the streets, help them learn new trades or just indulge their hobbies.

All the pupils were divided into four houses. During the year we were awarded points both for scholastic and sporting endeavour and at the end of the year the team with the most points won the school cup for that year. The four houses were: Kiwis (blue), Beavers (green), Springboks (yellow) and Kangaroos (red). With this being an obvious nod to our magnificent Empire, it was no surprise that the big occasion of the school year was Empire Day.

We celebrated this in the girls' playground as it was bigger than the boys'. The whole school assembled there to give praise to the Lord for giving us this mighty Empire, whose citizens were all proud to be British subjects. We all brought along a Union flag, which cost a ha'penny each. One of the older girls would be dressed as Britannia seated in a school chair on a raised dais. Such a magnificent sight that no wonder all our colonial subjects were so proud to be British.

The headmaster would then give a speech, extolling the virtues of our glorious Empire upon which the sun never set. We then sang a few songs and waved our flags. After this came the part we were all waiting for – the announcement of a half day holiday.

CHAPTER TWELVE

MILK CANS, BAGWASH AND MECHANICAL CLOWNS, 1926–9

'Oi, Ikey.' Mr Bellancoff, who lived on the floor below us, caught hold of me one day as I was on my way up to our flat, 'I'd like a word with you.' Mr Bellancoff was the local milkman and I wondered what I had done wrong. I racked my brains but couldn't think of how I might have upset him. 'Come in,' he said, showing me through his door. 'I've seen you around and you look like a bright lad.' 'Thank you,' I muttered, hoping this might lead to a penny or some sweets. However, what he was leading up to was something very different. 'How would you like to come and work for me?' he asked. I was a bit taken aback. Because we were always so close to the breadline, I knew that sooner or later I would be expected to find a job to help out with the family finances, but I hadn't thought it would be just yet. After all I was only eleven years old. Still, this could be my chance and mean a bit of much-needed extra money going into the Jacobs coffers, so I replied, 'Yeh, all right.' 'OK. Well, go and ask your mother and if it's all right with her, I'll see you in the morning. You know where my yard is, don't you?' I nodded. I had seen his milk churns many times outside no.4 Cleeve Workshops, a row of shops and workplaces just at the back of Cleeve Buildings, the block next to Sunbury.

I ran upstairs and threw our door open, 'Mum, Mum,' I yelled excitedly, 'Mr Bellancoff has just offered me a job. Can I do it?' Mum looked a bit startled then smiled and said, 'Do you want to do it?' I nodded. 'Well, of course, it's all right with your dad and me,' she replied.

The next morning found me up and out of the house by five o'clock and round to the yard. Although it was very early, it looked as though Mr Bellancoff had been there for some time. It was a bitterly cold morning and I felt very apprehensive. On the milk cart was a large golden churn surrounded by lots of smaller half-pint and one-pint milk cans. There was also a pail with a lid and two measures used to fill the cans. The system was to fill the cans from the pail, which was itself filled from the golden churn.

We set out from Cleeve, pushing the cart by hand round to all the Buildings in turn. When we got to each entrance, Mr Bellancoff would go off one way and I would go off the other, leaving a full can outside each door and bringing back the empty one that the flat owner had left out.

When we finished the round and got back, that was when the really hard work began as I had to scrub out all the returned cans and everything else we had used. I finished at 8.30, just in time to go home for breakfast, usually a couple of slices of bread and marge, or, if Dad was in work, maybe a couple of slices of bread and dripping, and a cup of tea sweetened with Goat Brand condensed milk. Then, after having done what seemed a full day's work already, it was off to school.

I stayed in this job for about two months till one day Dad came home one evening and said he had just found a new job as a French-polisher with a Mr Pollock, a maker of mahogany bookcases and bureaux just off Shoreditch High Street, and asked me if I would like to come and help him out after school. He said Mr Pollock had offered me 2s. 6d. a week, the same as I was getting from Mr Bellancoff. I jumped at the chance as first, I would be working with my dad, and secondly, I wouldn't have to get up early on cold mornings.

Having given Mr Bellancoff a week's notice, I duly arrived at Pollock's the following Monday after school, after first going home to collect Dad's tea – tea in a sterilised milk bottle and some sandwiches. There was a big open fire in the shop and we sat round this till he finished it.

Then I was introduced to Mr Pollock, who dispensed with all pleasantries and just said, 'Your father will show you what to do,' and walked off. Dad then made up a bucket of wood stain and told me I had to stain the bureau that was sitting in the workshop, top, sides and front, wipe it dry with a piece of canvas then fill it in with plaster of Paris. This was achieved by placing a wet rag in the plaster and rubbing it firmly into the grain of the wood. When it dried out and went white it was ready for the next stage. This involved dipping a rag into some linseed oil, rubbing it into the plaster till the colour was restored, sandpapering it and then wiping it dry with some more canvas.

'Bloody hell, Dad,' I said, about halfway through this process, 'can I have a rest?' My arms were aching so much that I wondered what had hit me. This was hard work, much harder even than cleaning out Mr Bellancoff's milk cans. Dad's only response was, 'Watch your language.' I managed to persevere through my suffering and eventually finished preparing my first bureau, because this was only the initial part of the process, which was called padding-up. After that, the first full coat of polish went on. I wasn't allowed to do this as it had to be done by a real craftsman.

Fortunately not all the jobs I was asked to do were as hard as this. Sometimes I just had to varnish the inside of the drawers. I was also often sent out on errands to buy the polish and other accessories necessary for the work, such as linseed oil, beeswax, white rags, wadding and so on. One thing I was never asked to buy was the brushes used to put the polish on with as it took a lot of experience to recognise a good brush.

Leading up to Christmas, when we were very busy, I even took a couple of days off school to help out. At this period, Dad sometimes stayed till eleven at night, or, even, on a couple of occasions, till midnight, but he would never let me stay beyond seven o'clock. At least with Dad's overtime and my contribution, it allowed us to have a decent Christmas.

Because I knew a bit about French polishing I also sometimes did a bit of work for a man called Len Manly at the weekends. Once he had to polish up a hundred billiard cues for a warehouse in Houndsditch and he asked me to deliver them on a barrow.

After the Christmas rush was over, it wasn't just Dad who was back on the unemployment register as I lost my job as well. After a couple of months I happened to be passing the laundry in Old Nichol Street one Saturday morning when Mrs Posner, the manageress, called me inside. 'You look like a strong lad,' she said. 'Do you think you can take four bags of washing to some houses in Hoxton for me?' I demurred a bit, but she said, 'There's a shilling in it for you.' That was all the encouragement I needed. She gave me a tanner and said, 'Taken this to Melandines and get a barrow, bring it back here and we'll load up the washing.'

Melandines was actually a greengrocer in Virginia Road, near my school, but they also had a sideline in hiring out barrows at sixpence an hour. I returned with my barrow, loaded up and off I went with the promise of a shilling when I returned. Hoxton was some way away, but I saw it as quite an adventure, having to cross the busy Kingsland Road with the trams going up and down. The occupants of each house I delivered to gave me a penny for my trouble, so that was an extra fourpence. When I returned to the laundry I was duly given my shilling and I ran home to give it to Mum, keeping the fourpence for myself.

'Look, Mum,' I said, excitedly. 'I've got a shilling for you.' She eyed me very suspiciously and said, 'Where d'you get that from?' I explained about my laundry delivery. She thought a bit and then instead of being pleased with my shilling, she had a blue fit and just exploded, 'What the 'ell does she think she's doing sending you all the way to 'Oxton 'cross Kingsland Road. You could 'ave been killed. You wait till I get my 'ands on the old bugger.' I was a bit taken aback with this reaction as I thought I had done something good. 'Don't say anything to her, Mum,' I pleaded. 'I'm sure she only thought she was doing something good, helping me earn a bit of money.' Mum calmed down a little and said, 'The lazy *nebbish*, she should 'ave gawn 'erself. Still, it's done now, but don't you ever do anything like that again without asking me first, Ikey, d'you 'ear?' I nodded and escaped with my fourpence to console myself with some sweets.

My next little money-making venture came when Aunt Hannah, Mum's sister, came to visit. She brought with her a box full of small mechanical wind-up toys, in the form of clowns. After Mum had made her a cup of tea, Hannah said to her, 'Would it be all right if your Ikey helped me by selling a few of these clowns down Bethnal Green Market?' Not one to hold back, Mum replied by saying, 'What's wrong with your own boys? A bit beneath 'em, is it?' Aunt Hannah had six boys including one about my age. Aunt Hannah made some lame excuse about them not feeling well, to which Mum's response was, 'What, all of them? Pull the other one, Hannah.' However, she looked at me and asked if I would like to do it. It sounded like a bit of a lark to me and anything a bit different that might earn me some money was OK by me, so I nodded and said, 'Yeh, I'll have a go.' The clowns were to be sold for sixpence each, with a penny from each sale for me.

And so, Saturday afternoon found me outside Lennard's, a shop that sold dairy produce, in the middle of Bethnal Green Market. The whole place was alive with hawkers, pedlars and stallholders shouting their wares with naphtha lamps spitting out flames above the stalls. There were shops illuminated and decorated, while throngs of people were weaving in and out between the stalls. I had a very limited space to exhibit my wares and I didn't sell many, but I had a good time caught up in the atmosphere of the place and earned a little bit of cash, so I was quite happy.

CHAPTER THIRTEEN

COWS, FRIED FISH AND PIERROTS, 1926–9

'Mum, Dad,' I shouted, throwing open the door after school one day, 'I've got a letter for you. Mr Wiggins said I had to give it to you as soon as I got home.'

'Oy-yoy-yoy, Ikey,' Mum said. 'What 'ave you done now?' She took the letter, ripped it open and read it. 'Look, Jack,' she said, handing the letter to Dad. 'They want to know if we're 'appy for Ikey to go on 'oliday.'

I was eleven years old and, of course, we had never been on a family holiday as we were far too poor. So this was my first chance to go away for a week. The holiday was being arranged through the school by a body called the Country Holiday Fund, a charitable organisation that had been set up for the express purpose of giving poor children a week's holiday in the country to get them out of the dirt and grime of London and breathe some wholesome air.

Mum and Dad didn't consider for long as they thought it would be good for me (and good for them too as they would have one less mouth to feed for a week!). 'Do you want to go, Ikey?' Dad asked. I was very excited by the prospect and immediately replied, 'Yes, can I?' Dad nodded and said, 'Of course.'

Then Mum thought of a snag. 'Jack,' she said, 'if Ikey's going to the country to live amongst posh people [she thought that everyone living in the country must be posh], we can't let them think 'is name is Ikey.'

'Why ever not?' said Dad.

'Well, it's a bit common, isn't it?'

Dad shook his head and took an extra long drag on his cigarette before asking, 'Well, what do you suggest then?'

Mum thought a bit and then came up with the name Alf. 'I think we should say 'is name is Alf, that sounds a bit more respectable.' Dad just laughed. Nevertheless, I was instantly renamed Alf and ever since then that's how I have been known, even after I returned to the Buildings from my holiday. From that day on, Ikey no longer existed.

On the morning of departure we were told to report to the Cambridge Heath and Bethnal Green Jewish Boys' Club, our parents having been given a list of items we had to take with us, including sandwiches for the journey, some clothes and a toothbrush, which had to be bought specially for the holiday as we never used them at home. Mum took me to the meeting place, repeatedly telling me to 'be a good boy' – as if I would be anything else! When I met up with the rest of the party I found them all to be Jewish boys and girls from the Buildings, so I knew most of them.

Our first adventure was to take the Underground from Old Street to London Bridge, my first experience of the tube. It seemed very strange to me. Nothing to see out the window except black walls until suddenly you'd come into a station and everything was very light. I can't say I was too impressed.

Once at London Bridge we were all counted to make sure everyone had got off the Underground and then made our way to the platform to get the overground train to Tunbridge Wells in faraway Kent. Buzzing with excitement, we all piled on to the train. Each compartment had a designated adult or an older child to look after its young inhabitants. We were looked after by a sixteen-year-old girl I knew from the Buildings called Hilda Bruckner, ably assisted by her fourteen-year-old sister, Hetty. Their brother, Izzy, was in my class at school.

I was lucky enough to get a seat in the corner by the window. As the train started off I had my nose pressed hard against the pane, looking out at this new world that was opening up in front of me as rails, signals, trains and houses flashed by. This was the life and I forgot all about the Buildings with its stacked-up flats and workshops. Although Hilda forbade us to open the windows, once we were out in the country I couldn't help defying her orders so as to get a smell of the fresh air. 'Ikey, shut that window!' she shouted. 'My name's Alf,' I replied. The other boys in the carriage laughed. 'Alf?' repeated Benny, a boy in my class. 'Since when?' 'My mum said I'm to be called Alf from now on,' I replied defiantly. 'OK, if you say so, Alf,' laughed Benny, putting a heavy emphasis on my new name.

After a while, along with everyone else it seemed, I decided it was time for a sandwich. There was a general clatter as our small cases were pulled down from the overhead luggage racks and packages of sandwiches extracted. Mine was a jam sandwich; this in itself seemed to show I was on holiday as I had expected just the normal bread and marge. For the next few minutes we all munched away happily amid much merriment and chatter.

Eventually we arrived at Tunbridge Wells station after passing through a very long tunnel. In those days tunnels were quite a hazard and windows had to be pulled up and closed tightly, otherwise the carriage would be filled with the black smoke and grit that was belched out of the funnel. In spite of our best efforts however, by the time we arrived I had grit in both my eyes and smudges on my face and looked a bit like a street urchin instead of the respectable Alf Mum was hoping would impress the posh people of Kent.

After being marshalled off the train, lined up and accounted for, we boarded a charabanc and were taken to a hall in a nearby village called Southborough, where, waiting to receive us, were a number of women. As we lined up, one woman came over to me and said, 'You, come with me.' So I left the line to join her. She did this with three other boys and, after being satisfied with her selection, she marched us off down the road to her house where she lived with her husband and brother. We later learnt her name was Mrs King.

When we arrived she gave us each a small card with an address written on it. 'If you have any questions or, God forbid, complaints, you are to go this address,' she said. Then added, 'Also, you will go there at midday every day to collect your lunch. Now then, go and put your cases in your rooms, wash your hands and come back here for tea.' Her husband led us up the stairs and showed us two rooms, two boys to a room. I bunked in with Jerry Barnett, a boy in my class at school. I couldn't believe the luxury of this place. There were four rooms upstairs and our room even had a jug with water in and a basin with some soap. Imagine, just two to a room with soap and water. These people must be unbelievably rich was my main thought. We had a quick wash and then raced downstairs for our tea.

Once again what faced us was so different from our everyday experience. There on the table were four places set out with china plates, all the same design, four cups and saucers (not cracked jam jars but real cups) as well as four linen napkins. In the middle of the table there was a large plate with a number of slices of bread and jam and another with some rock cakes on it. There was a silver teapot, a sugar bowl with sugar cubes and sugar tongs, a milk jug and another jug with hot water in it. Even Ada Bloom didn't run to this sort of opulence. I wondered for a moment if these people were Royalty or at least Lord and Lady Somebody.

After tea, Mrs King told us to write to our parents on the stamped addressed postcards we had been given before leaving that morning to let them know we had arrived safe and sound. Once she had gathered these up we all retired to bed after a very hectic and busy day. I don't know about the others, but as soon as my head hit the pillow I was fast asleep.

It was a very strange feeling waking up in the morning to find yourself in a strange place, in somebody else's house. The first thing that struck me as soon as I properly came to and realised where I was, was the quiet. Back in the Buildings, there was always continuous noise and action. What with six young brothers and sisters all clattering around and making their own noise and Mum and Dad urging us to get ready for school or shopping or whatever and the thin walls through which you could often hear the neighbours, there was a continuous clamour and hubbub, something which, of course, we were perfectly used to and took no notice of. It was this peace and quiet that was so strange. Peace and quiet that is, until Jerry woke up and hurled his pillow at me, saying, ''Ere this is a bit of all right, ain't it, Ikey?' 'Alf,' I reminded him. 'OK, Alf,' laughed Jerry. 'But, yeh, it is,' I replied.

After a luxurious breakfast of cornflakes and toast and jam we were told to go out and 'enjoy the fresh air'. We were not expected to come back until lunchtime when we would bring back our packed lunches and eat them at the table, then go out again until it was time to come back for tea. The idea behind these holidays being that we got as much fresh air in our lungs as possible to try and drive out the accumulated dirt and grime of the London air we had been brought up on.

As we walked along the road I couldn't help but notice that all the front gardens were ablaze with colour; flowers of all descriptions growing in abundance. Unfortunately a few of the gardens contained lavender plants in their display. I had to give these gardens a wide berth as for some reason the smell of lavender always gave me a splitting headache.

At the bottom of the road was a small general store, which naturally we thought we ought to explore, so we called in and spent nearly all the money we had been given on sweets. Just beyond the shop we found a small field, so we went there and had a run around, played tag and climbed up a couple of the trees that stood round its far edge.

At lunchtime we went to the address on the card to pick up our lunches. They were wrapped up in paper and we were told not to open them until we got back to our lodgings. Once back there, we all opened our parcels and found some fried fish inside. Mrs King put these on plates for us and gave us all a cup of tea. After we finished it was back out again until tea time.

Our lunch consisted of fried fish every day, so, nice as it was, it got a bit boring. It did occur to me at the time that maybe they gave us fish every day because they were a bit unsure of how to deal with a group of Jewish children and were concerned that if they gave us meat it might not be kosher, so they settled for the safe option.

The following day we made a beeline for the shop again, but on reaching it, I realised I only had a penny left, so when we got back for lunch I asked Mrs King if I could have a postcard as I wanted to write and let my nan know I was well and enjoying myself. As it was in such a good cause, Mrs King didn't seem to mind giving me a card and a stamp. If she'd known what I really wanted it for I'm not so sure she would have handed them over so readily. I wrote on the postcard, 'Dear Nanny, I am having a nice holiday, but have only got one penny left. Love, Alf.' This card had the desired effect and two days later a letter arrived for me sent by Nan and enclosing six one-penny stamps. I was able to use these stamps as currency in the general store. I was later told that my postcard was the cause of much laughter for many a long day in my grandparents' house.

The novelty of living away from home and in the fresh country air began to wear off after a couple of days. We really found ourselves at a loose end as there was nothing organised and we were just left to our own devices every day. The shop and the field had their attractions, but they did get a bit boring when that was all there was to do. So that when the time came to leave our Kentish haven, I was ready for it. I was missing my home and family and the familiar surroundings of the Buildings – I was never at a loose end there.

The following year, I went on another holiday courtesy of the same fund. This time to the seaside at Weymouth. I was 'billeted' with just one other boy, Johnny Saunders, with Mr and Mrs Haines. All the arrangements were much the same as before except that this was a much smaller house and Johnny and I had to share a bed.

Weymouth itself was a revelation to me. It was the first time I had ever seen the sea. The beaches, some sandy, some stony, stretched for miles, this was incredible for a boy whose only contact with a beach before had been the one down by Tower Bridge at the side of the Thames.

On one of the sandy beaches was a real live Pierrot show with the performers wearing white costumes, ruffs, big black pom-poms, the lot. It was a mixed troupe and the men and women all took their turn singing and dancing and playing out small comedy sketches. There was also a piano and pianist. All of this on a stage enclosed within two side walls, a roof and a covered back. I'd never seen anything like it in all my life. I returned every day to see these stars of the local stage. Now this was more like a holiday!

I have never forgotten those Pierrots or their signature song:

> If you don't like milk and honey,
> Where the skies are always sunny,
> If you don't like folks that say 'howd' ya do'
> Stay out of the south!

When this holiday came to an end I was much more reluctant to leave, but like all good things, sadly, it did have to end. It would be a very long time before I was to see the sea again. But I was never again to see a Pierrot show on the sands, its rightful place.

CHAPTER FOURTEEN

CLICKY-BA, NOAH'S ARK AND THE MUSIC HALL, 1926–9

As I grew up I began to lose my interest in comics – they were kid's stuff – and started to read more, beginning with paper story books – called 'story papers' – like *The Wizard*, *The Rover* and *Adventure*, in whose pages one could meet such characters as Morgan the Mighty, Cast Iron Bill, the Wolf of Kabul, and Chang, whose awesome weapon was a cricket bat, which he called clicky-ba. My favourite though was the Black Sapper, who rode around in a sort of land submarine. Whenever he wanted to go somewhere he would get in his long cylindrical machine, bore down into the ground with the two long drills attached to the front, travel underground and emerge at the place he wanted to go to.

The shop I bought these story papers was in Virginia Road and was a very old dilapidated shop, the inside of which was very dirty and untidy, and was run by an old lady called Esther, who had very similar characteristics to that of the shop. The reason I used this shop was because she sold the magazines at half price as they were a week old. She'd buy them in from the boys who had bought them new elsewhere for a ha'penny and sell them on for a penny.

From these I progressed to *The Magnet* and *The Gem*, both of which contained stories about public schools, the most famous being Greyfriars revolving around the school days of Billy Bunter, 'the Fat Owl of The Remove', who, even to this day, is no doubt still waiting for his postal order to arrive from Bunter Towers.

I also started going out to the cinema more. The Cambridge was still a favourite, but I was more aware now of my journey to get there as this was through Wheeler Street Arch, which ran underneath the main railway line into Liverpool Street from Bishopsgate to Commercial Street. Once through the arch though, I came out to one of my favourite spots, the transport yard belonging to Knellor and Chandler. As well as motor transport there were always two or three steam traction engines there. When they were working they were a fine site to behold, smoke pouring out of their funnels and hot ashes falling into a large tray below.

It was a bit scary coming home in the evening when it got dark though, as the left-hand side had a recess in it and it was here that all the down-and-outs and homeless spent the night with whatever cover they could muster. If I had just seen a Lon Chaney film it was even worse. Surely one of these down-and-outs was one of the frightful monsters he had been playing and was just waiting to leap out and grab me. Of course none ever did and these poor unfortunate people were even worse off than we were and I had to run the gauntlet of them begging for money, but that we might have some spare money to give them was completely out of the question.

As well as the Cambridge, the Olympia started to become more attractive the older I got, with its 'grown-up' films. They also had live acts on stage between films. It was at the Olympia that I saw my first talkie, *Noah's Ark*. It started as a silent movie but halfway through the film the actors started talking.

There were a number of other local cinemas I occasionally went to, including Smart's in Bethnal Green Road, the Grand Central in Hackney Road and the Standard in Goldsmith's Row. There was also a well-known music hall in Shoreditch High Street, called the London. Its posters outside would portray the different turns appearing there and included some of the big names of the time, including Sam Mayo, Wilkie Bard and Wee Georgie Wood. I was fortunate enough to see a few of these turns before the theatre closed and was demolished in the mid-1930s. One vivid memory I still have of visiting this music hall was seeing Rosie Lloyd, Marie Lloyd's sister, singing a song that ended with the words, 'So I'm going to take the sunlight back' and then, from behind her back, she produced an overgrown bar of Sunlight soap.

Up the side of the London there ran a long alleyway to the rear of the building, outside which stood two large dustbins. One day I was with my friend Hymie Marcovitch, when, for some reason, he decided to take a look inside one of the dustbins. He took the lid off and peered in. He turned to me and said, 'Alf, there's only a load of fuckin' programmes in 'ere.'

I looked in and we pulled a few out. 'These are for this week's show,' I said. Many were torn or grubby, which is presumably why they were thrown away, but some were not too bad.

''Ere,' Hymie said, holding one of the not-too-bad programmes, 'we could flog these.' I inspected it and nodded my head. And so we decided to go into the programme business. We pulled out all the programmes and sorted them out, keeping the cleaner ones and putting back those too bad to be sold on. That night we sold them to the galleryites, the people in the cheap seats who always had to line up outside while the posher customers in the dearer seats walked straight in. About half an hour before going-in time we walked along the ever-growing queue offering our programmes for 1d. as against the official price of 2d.

For a few days we had a nice business going until other boys discovered what we were doing and muscled in, spoiling it for us. Ah well, that's show business!

Another live performance I looked forward to every year was the Annual Pantomime at the Hackney Radical Club. Aunt Leah and her husband, Uncle Johnnie, were members. Every year Aunt Leah would come up to the school and bail all us Jacobses out early. Then she travelled with us by tram up to Median Road in Lower Clapton, where it was a short walk through to the club in Dunlace Road. After the show, on the way out, we were all given a brown paper bag containing fruit and sweets and a new penny. Dad used to meet us as we came out and, after another tram journey, we'd all arrive safely back at the Buildings.

I also regularly used to attend the concerts at the Metropolitan

Working Men's Club in Cambridge Road. These were for members and their families only. The turns used to get 2s. 6d. per song and usually sang three songs. Comedians and magicians would get 7s. 6d. for their act as well. It was here that I first heard the song, 'Are you Lonesome Tonight?', later made famous by Elvis Presley of course.

The reason I was able to go here was because since moving to the Buildings, Dad had changed his allegiance from the Netherlands Club to this one, which was a lot nearer. From his time at the Netherlands Club and now the Metropolitan, Dad became a very proficient billiards and snooker player. In spite of living on the bread line, he managed to buy himself a very nice cue and metal case to put it in. I was at the club the night one of Britain's leading professional players, William Cook Junior, who, at the time, held the world record for the highest billiards break, put in an appearance at the club to play an exhibition match. As the best player at the club, Dad was chosen to represent them in the match. Of course he lost, but it was a big honour to be chosen to play one of the best billiards players of all time.

As it happens I shouldn't have been there as youngsters under the age of sixteen were forbidden to go into the club, as Aubrey the doorman told me before letting me in with a wink. I visited several times more with Dad, always with Aubrey giving me a knowing wink. He once gave me a small pocket book called, *Hoyle's Games*, which set out the rules to many card games and other board games such as chess and backgammon. Even at that time the book was over a hundred years old and we have it in our family to this day.

CHAPTER FIFTEEN

SHEEP'S HEADS AND PIG'S TROTTERS, 1926–9

'Alf, take the basin along to Garrett's and get some saveloys and pease pudding for tea.' This was an oft-repeated cry in our house as Mum considered what we should have that night. Garrett's was our local butcher and stood next to Fitt's Eel and Pie Shop on the corner of Brick Lane. The shop used to open up in the evening especially for saveloys, faggots and pease pudding, which would be served up hot and steaming. During the day they sold such delicacies as sheep's heads and pigs' trotters. These were very cheap so we partook of them on many occasions.

Our move to Arnold Circus meant we had to find new shops. Our main shopping street was now Brick Lane. My favourite shop was Kosolofsky, the sweet shop. They had two types of lucky dip. The first was in the form of a small thin stick of rock.

This cost a halfpenny. If on breaking it you found a red dot inside, you won 2 ounces of toffees. The second was you paid a halfpenny and selected an envelope from a big box. Inside the envelope was a card which had printed on it the amount of toffee you were entitled to. This ranged from ½ oz to ¼ lb. No prizes for guessing the most frequent weight to appear! If you just wanted to buy toffees, they cost 2d. per ¼ lb.

Next door was Leboff's, the haberdasher. Girls used to go here to buy their hair ribbons. Every girl wore ribbons in their hair at that time. They later changed their name to Fobel and expanded into the timber trade and DIY accessories, lasting until well after the Second World War, with branches all over the country.

A little further down was Berdovsky the baker. It was in his shop that I saw my first-ever slicing machine, worked manually by turning a handle at the side. It cost ½d for this service. It was here we sometimes bought cake. Seedy cake with caraway seeds and currant cake were the two most affordable and therefore our most frequent purchases. The dearer ones we sometimes managed to run to were cheesecake, a heavy firm cake, light inside and brown outside, and apple strudel, my favourite.

There was another baker. Nordheim's, in Brick Lane. This was where we now bought our stale bread when times were a bit rough.

A little further down was the Jolly Butchers pub, well frequented by the market traders themselves. Just further on, Brick Lane became part of the infamous Club Row Sunday Dog Market, together with a few of the side streets. Dogs of all breeds and sizes were bought and sold here, probably amidst much cruelty as they always seemed to be very thin and bony and kept in very cramped conditions. These unlucky animals were the products of backyard breeders in the main, who were much more interested in a small profit than animal welfare.

One of the side roads involved in this trade was Sclater Street and going down there from Brick Lane was a well-known bird and seed shop called (appropriately) Fowler's. They stocked hundreds of birds from linnets to parrots and sold a variety of cages from a stall outside. I often looked in here just to see all the bright colours on the birds and to hear them singing or, in the case of the parrots, talking.

Opposite Fowler's was the stall of Alf Valentine, the 'Purse King'. He was one of the great East End characters. Crowds would gather around him just to hear his patter, which went something like this. He'd hold up a purse or handbag and say, 'Look at this, ladies, real leather. Can't be beaten. I went to Africa specially to get the animal skins to make these myself. I went with my friend, Louis. We were out in the jungle one day when Louis says to me, "I'll take your photo, Alf, do you want it taken long or short?" Just at that moment I saw a lion so I was taken short. Real leather. Can't be beaten. Cost in the shops, 'alf a crown. You can get it 'ere for a tanner. Who's first? Form an orderly queue. I've got enough for everyone. It was a very big lion.' Alf would carry on like this all morning interspersing his sales patter with his little jokes. The crowd would lap it up and he did a good trade.

Another well-known stall along that stretch of the road belonged to the 'Pencil Man'. He sold a handful of pencils for a penny. They were all used, from stubs to almost new.

He had thousands of them spread all over this stall. One day, when I was about twelve, I stood watching him, when he called me over and said, "Ow d'ye fancy earning a few coppers?" Always eager to boost my exchequer, I nodded. 'Right then,' he continued, 'look after this stall for a little while. I've got some urgent business to see to.' I managed to sell a few handfuls and when he returned from his urgent business, which I suspect was a trip down to the Jolly Butchers, I gave him what I had earned and he gave me threepence. I carried on with this job for a couple of months. Then one day I went down there and he wasn't there and I never saw him again. By this time I had a sizeable collection of pencils as he always gave me a few each week as well as my threepence. My favourites were the indelible ones. You licked the point before writing with them and they wrote like ink.

A popular feature of Brick Lane market was the escapologist who performed at the mouth of Wheeler Street Arch. He would stand on his pitch, with a big sign above his head which he fixed to the wall, proclaiming that here was 'Howdini, King of the Escape Artists'. When a big enough crowd had gathered to make it worth his while he would start his spiel, 'Good morning. Come closer. My name is Howdini, no relation to that other famous escape artist of a similar name, just better! What I am about to do will amaze and astound you. You will not believe it and will still be telling your grandchildren about me in fifty years' time.' As most of the crowd were probably well into their forties or fifties at least this claim seemed highly improbable and usually got a good laugh. 'Now I want four strong gentlemen to come forward to help me.' He would then point to people in the crowd and ask them to come forward. 'Now,' he continued, 'you see all those straps, chains and padlocks on the pavement? I want you to pick them up and bind me tightly in them. So tightly that escape would be impossible.' He then allowed himself to be strapped, chained and padlocked by his four chosen members of the public till he could hardly be seen for metal. Well, at least he said the chains and padlocks were solid metal and why should he lie? Once the helpers were satisfied that they'd made it impossible for him to free himself from the chains, he thanked them for their help and went on, 'I know you all think I will never escape from these bonds, and maybe you are right, but if you will all kindly throw some money into my hat, I will see what I can do. But I have to warn you now, no money, no escape!' By now everyone was itching to see how he could possibly get out of this mass of ironware that fully enclosed him, so they threw coppers and even the odd bit of silver into his hat which he had placed on the ground in front. When he was satisfied that he had extracted all he was likely to extract from the audience, the contortions and gyrations, puffing and panting commenced until lo and behold at his feet lay this mighty mass of metal that had encumbered him barely ten minutes before. There was a big round of applause while Howdini went off to the Jolly Butchers for a well-earned drink and rest. About forty minutes later he would be back performing his escape.

Columbia Road Flower Market was another well-known local market. There were stalls on both sides of the road full of plants of all descriptions. Many's the time I used part of my 3d. from the pencil man to buy fuchsias, petunias or geraniums for Mum's window box.

Nearby, at the Virginia Road end of Columbia Market, was the Bell Coffee Shop, run by old George Read, his son George and daughter-in-law, Letty. Old George was a bit of a character and would regale anyone who went in for a coffee with his tales of the Boer War. 'Have I ever told you about the time, Lord Baden-Powell himself asked me to take a message down the line to one of his generals? The general had got caught out with a small platoon and had come under heavy fire from the Boers. I had to get him the message to let him know help was on its way. But, of course, I came under heavy fire myself. Luckily I managed to dodge round the bullets and get the message through.' It was never quite clear, but it seemed Old George had been a messenger of some sort and all his messages seemed to involve him running the gauntlet through a hail of bullets or some such. I'm not sure we believed all his stories, but they certainly livened up a cup of coffee.

Another local street, Mount Street, had a number of factories and shops. One, in particular I remember was Vavasseur, the last remaining Huguenot weavers in an area they had once dominated.

We bought our fresh fish from Johnny Hughes in Mount Street. His stall was closed in rather than open like most of them were and looked more like a little shed. One day Mum bought some plaice there and when we got them home, she tipped them out on to the table. Julie, who was in the kitchen helping Mum get the dinner ready, looked at them and gave a loud scream. Mum and I turned to see what the matter was and we saw Julie pointing at the fish. 'They're alive!' she yelped.

'Alf, get a bowl of water, quick,' Mum commanded. So I

got a bowl, filled it up with water and Mum picked the fish up and put them into it. Julie meanwhile ran out of the room still screaming. As they flipped about in the water we saw their mouths open and shut. I was wondering to myself if maybe we could keep them as pets. However, it was not to be as they were to be fried within the hour, so their reprieve was short lived.

A little further down, Johnny Hughes also had a proper shop, but this specialised in dried, smoked and cured fish rather than the wet fish on his stall. His most popular lines were smoked haddock, kippers and hard roe bloaters, which were Dad's favourite and, when funds allowed, he would often have for his tea. At the back of the shop was a large round tin containing anchovies preserved in salt. We'd also buy tinned fish here, such as Marie Elizabeth sardines, William Bruce tomato herrings and Sailor Salmon.

For ready-made fish and chips we'd call in at Jack's, who was reputed to be the best fish and chip shop in the East End. A tuppenny bit and a penn'orth was the standard order. If we had any spare cash, a wally (gherkin) was obtained from a large glass jar on the counter for a penny.

For some reason, smoked salmon was not available at the fishmongers, but rather bought at the nearby delicatessen, Piper's. Sadly it was well out of our range, but sometimes, when Dad had had a particularly good week, we might be able to afford smoked salmon cuttings – the remains left over after trimming the salmon and included the head, skin and other bits. These cuttings would be sold off in sixpenny- and one-shilling lots. What an absolute treat they were on the rare occasions we had them! Other fish that could be obtained at Piper's were pickled herrings served with lashings of onions, rollmops and Dutch herring. All good cheap food which, because of its low cost, played a large part in our diet.

Because of our continuing precarious financial position, fish was our staple diet rather than meat. As it happens I didn't mind this as I preferred fish to meat. I liked all fish, except, for some strange reason, mackerel. I could never quite come to terms with this particular seafaring creature. When we had some funds, we would find large dishes of plaice and haddock being fried, while at other times we might be lucky and get some sprats and herring. We usually had soused herring, which meant putting them into the oven soaked in vinegar with allspice and bay leaves.

Although I didn't like it very much, mackerel was done as a stew with eggs, lemons and onions being the chief ingredients. But, of course, beggars can't be choosers and I had to eat it or starve.

Gefilte fish was a Yiddisher delicacy. Haddock, though it could sometimes be cod, was cut in slices, all the fish scraped out, the skin being kept whole, the flesh chopped finely with grated carrots and onions, salt and pepper added, then put back into the skin and boiled with onions.

Plaice was normally poached in hot water then served with butter and pepper. I think this was my real favourite and it makes my mouth water even now just thinking about it!

Other items we bought from the delicatessen were pickled cucumbers, sauerkraut and red cabbage. These were all sold loose out of wooden tubs and you took your own basin along for the shopkeeper to shovel them into. If you went without a basin, they would be wrapped up for you in greaseproof paper and then in newspaper.

Piper's also specialised in cooked meats, including ham on the bone. This came in sixpenny portions and, if you managed to get there just as the last few slices were being cut, it was one of life's absolute luxuries and a rare treat. They also sold home-made brawn. This was made in a big bowl, turned out on to a marble slab and then cut to requirements. To say it was delicious would be too much of an understatement and far from doing this ambrosia of the gods justice.

Some other cheaper meals we had included wurst and eggs. The wurst would be fried with garlic and the eggs (normally the cracked ones) beaten and poured over the wurst while still in the pan. Onion omelette also made a nice cheap meal.

Finally, there was one more shopping street that ran off Brick Lane called Church Street. This contained a very long-established chemist, a kosher butcher and a newsagent. However, we used this street mostly because our panel doctor, Vivian Ridewood, had his practice there. He also had a resident apothecary, so all prescriptions were made up on the premises. Not that we went there that often if we could help it as, of course, in those days it cost money to see the doctor. So we mostly made do with either homemade remedies or cheap shop-bought popular brands. Mum swore by Carter's Little Liver Pills. It seemed to be her cure for everything from a headache to a nose bleed, from a cough to a stomach upset. Other available cure-alls included Kruschen Salts and Glauber Salts, while Germolene, Zam-Buk, Melrose and Vaseline were used for chapped hands; the latter was also incongruously used as a hair cream.

If we had an injury that couldn't be treated at home – and there were a number of those due to some rather strong tackles while playing football in the street or other rough games on the concrete playground at the Buildings – we'd be taken off to the Mildmay Mission Hospital, which fortunately was quite close. Should you turn up at their portals with anything less than a fatal injury, while a church service was in progress, you would have to wait until it finished. The worst injury I can remember any of us having whilst living in the Buildings, was when Joey broke his right radius falling off a wall he was trying to walk along. We belonged to the Hospital Savings Association, which cost a copper or two a week and allowed you mostly free treatment unless it was particularly complicated. I suppose Mum and Dad thought that what with seven kids all liable to cuts, bruises and grazes at any time, it was a prudent outlay.

After we'd been seen at the hospital, the doctor would invariably prescribe a tonic, which was nearly always Parrish's Food, a horrible-tasting thick red mixture. I believe most people felt a lot better just by pouring it down the sink and watching it disappear. The better-off would swear by Wincarnis or Hall's Wine, which was no doubt a tonic for their makers.

The local pawnshops always displayed the three brass balls above the window. The one I dealt with on Mum's behalf had its pledge entrance in Boundary Passage, while the shop entrance faced on to Shoreditch High Street. Presumably this was to separate the poor people like us, taking something in to pawn, from the wealthier customers who were coming in to buy.

The three brass balls above the pawnshops were a reminder of the days when all shops displayed some form of symbol to show what their trade was. This practice had largely died out by the 1920s, but two other types of business steadfastly stuck to these old ways. Those were the barbers, who advertised their presence with a red and white twisted-stripe pole by the door, and chemists who had their trademark shop sign, three or four large carboys filled with coloured water, on a shelf in the window.

Increasingly, a number of shops began to display a blue tin sign outside with the legend, 'You may telephone from here' inscribed on it. No one I knew had a telephone at home, so these shops could be handy if you wanted to phone someone. On the other hand, as no one we knew had a phone we never really needed this service anyway.

There was also a fair smattering of street vendors, mostly much the same as those who came round the Tenterground, though some were now being modernised. For example, ice-cream tricycles were superseding the old heavy ice-cream barrows. Eldorado and Walls, with its slogan 'Stop me and buy one', being two of the first to change to this new mode of transport.

One street vendor who came right into the Buildings them-selves was the beigel girl. She was one of those characters who defy description. I suppose she was about twenty years old, but dressed as though she was sixty. She pushed her wares around in an old pram, racing through the playground, screaming out at the top of her voice, 'Beigel! Fresh beigel!' You had to be quick if you wanted to stop her and buy anything off her. Her speed was such that it was almost as if she didn't actually want to sell any beigels, preferring to keep them all for herself. Truly a character the like of which we will never see again.

Other professional workers to be seen going about their business included the local policeman, who was always around ready to give a quick clip round the ear to any youngsters he thought were misbehaving. Still better that than have him report your misdemeanours to your parents. One thing police didn't have to deal with much in those days was illegally parked cars as there weren't any. There weren't any legally parked cars either as the streets were always completely free of any parked cars, because no one in the Buildings or nearby could afford one.

It was rare to see a policewoman in those days and those there were were generally made fun of by the local youth. Postmen were frequently about as there were a lot more deliveries then, something like three or four a day. They always wore a uniform with a double peaked cap, one at the front, one at the rear. When delivering they always rat-tatted on the knocker. The most feared person to knock on your door was the telegram boy as he was always considered to be the harbinger of bad news.

We were also near the centre of Shoreditch, about one or two minutes' walk from all the main buildings in that illustrious borough. Nearest of all was the very well-known and popular landmark, St Leonard's Church, generally known as Shoreditch Church of the famous 'Oranges and Lemons' rhyme. Its part in that famous verse was to sing out, 'When I grow rich', which seemed very appropriate given the circumstances, not only of our family, but generally of those living round about. Designed in 1740 by George Dance the Elder, it firmly stood its ground and weathered all the changes going on around it between Calvert Avenue, Hackney Road and Shoreditch High Street and would send its bells pealing out at the least provocation, especially on Sunday mornings when we were trying to have a lie-in. In front of the church was a small park which had on display within its grounds a relic of bygone days, the stocks and whipping post.

Opposite the church was a big junction where four important roads, Shoreditch High Street, Hackney Road, Old Street and Kingsland Road met. As this was such a busy junction, there was always a policeman on point duty wearing a white armband, to direct the traffic. There were no traffic lights at that time in London, apart from some experimental lights just being introduced at Ludgate Circus. These were controlled by hand by a policeman sitting in a box in the middle of the junction.

This corner was also full of buses going every which way. The official London buses were then owned and run by the London General Omnibus Co., but 'pirate' buses were also an everyday sight. One in particular I remember was called 'Public' and used to follow General's 69 route down Shoreditch High Street from Edmonton to Camberwell Green. There was another company called Pro Bono Publico. General's bus drivers and conductors wore uniforms with peaked caps, which had a white cover over the crown in summer.

Shoreditch mainline railway station stood on the corner of Old Street and Kingsland Road, the gateway ready to transport you to such glamorous-sounding places as Watford, Kew Gardens and Richmond. Its main London terminus was Broad

Street, one station down the line and close to Liverpool Street Station. A little way past the station, proceeding up Old Street was our local police station. By its side, in the same building, stood Old Street Magistrates' Court, while facing this building, on the opposite side of the road, was the Town Hall.

Back in Shoreditch High Street, just along from the church, stood two big businesses, Jeremiah Rotherham and Hopkins and Pegg's. Rotherham's was a very long-established wholesale draper, which had originally come from Anlaby in Yorkshire in the mid-1900s, which is why they now called their building in Shoreditch, Anlaby House. Their premises went through to Boundary Street, where the loading bays dealt with the incoming and outgoing merchandise. In the 1930s, they bought the London Music Hall and demolished it to extend their expanding business.

Hopkins and Pegg had about half a dozen shops extending from Church Street (later Redchurch Street) to Bethnal Green Road. They were retail drapers, haberdashers and sold all the accompanying accessories for ladies. The shops were run most certainly on the Kipps principle. The staff would have to dress correctly and the majority slept on the premises. They closed down in the late 1920s or early 1930s, but not before they had given their name to a piece of cockney rhyming slang, Hopkins and Pegg's – legs, usually shortened to just Hopkins. On the other side of Church Street stood a large shop specialising in men's and boys' wear. Its fascia somewhat enigmatically proclaimed, 'Lynes from Opposite'.

Across Shoreditch High Street, opposite Barclay's Bank, was a branch of the Aerated Bread Company, known simply as the

ABC. This was a well-known chain of tea shops at one time rivalling Lyons' Corner Houses. Further down was the post office and then came R & J Hill, which stood on the corner of New Inn Yard with its premises extending down the latter. Hill's was a cigarette and tobacco manufacturers whose main brands were Sunripe and Spinet. Many and varied were the fag cards they issued. Crossing over Holywell Lane was the Olympia cinema. Outside the Olympia and spreading into the road itself stood a number of bookstalls where I would often go for a browse, though I couldn't really afford to buy many.

CHAPTER SIXTEEN

TWO-VALVE RADIO, THE CHAVRA MAN AND APPLE CAKE, 1926–9

'I've told you before, you fuckin' *momzer*, you leave my ol' woman alone, d'you fuckin' 'ear me?'

Grandpa took a quick look out the window to confirm what he already knew: 'Peggy's back then,' he announced matter-of-factly to the room. No one took much notice.

'Oi, I said d'you 'ear me, you fucker?' Peggy continued his shrieking outside the house next door.

Nanny looked up and muttered, 'You'd think a man of his age would know better than to make such a spectacle of himself in the street.'

'Come out 'ere and fuckin' face me, you schmuck. I'll learn you to *yentz* my missis.'

Nanny and Grandpa seemed to find this last remark particularly amusing.

''E'll learn 'im? I wonder what he's gonna do about it then, the ole cripple,' laughed Grandpa.

'P'raps he'll take off one of his wooden legs and bash Woolfy over the head with it!' Nanny opined. This set Grandpa off laughing so loudly that it wasn't long before his heavy smoking habit caught up with him and he almost collapsed in a paroxysm of coughing and fighting for air.

Peggy's ranting and the continued amusement and mocking from Nanny and Grandpa, not to mention his rasping cough, went on for some time before, receiving no response, the street abuser finally gave up and went away.

This scene, or something like it, was a fairly regular occurrence on my Sunday visits to Nanny and Grandpa's house in Gateshead Place in Mile End. Often I would ask who this man was, but I was just told he was not a very nice man and I shouldn't listen to him, though that was very hard to do considering how loud he always shouted.

Sometimes, but not that often I would visit Uncle Woolfy, who lived in the house next door, and was apparently the object of Peggy's outraged abuse. My only real memory of him at this time was that he constantly seemed to be bathing both his feet in a bowl of water placed on the floor of the living room. He told me he had to do this regularly owing to some problem he had with his toes which were very dark brown in colour, the consequence of some incident or other whilst serving in the Navy during the First World War.

The other main thing I remember about my visits was that Betsy, his wife, would always be going on about some woman called 'Becontree Annie'. After a while it became clear to me that my wayward uncle was paying court to this woman from the Essex countryside and this was what all the shouting was about as the man shouting profanities outside in the street was none other than Becontree Annie's husband, Abraham Joseph, aka Peggy. Now Uncle Woolfy having an affair with Peggy's wife would be bad enough, but what made this situation even worse was that Uncle Woolfy's wife, Betsy, was Peggy's sister, so he therefore had double reason to be outraged with Uncle Woolfy's behaviour. Yet, in spite of this, whenever he came round, Nanny and Grandpa, instead of remonstrating with their wayward son, defended him and mocked poor old Abraham, who, to add to his woes, was a cripple who had had both his legs amputated and now relied on his two wooden legs and a pair of crutches to get around, hence the nickname Peggy.

These outbursts punctuated what had become my normal Sunday routine since moving to the Buildings as it was about that time that I was deemed old enough to go off and visit Nanny and Grandpa, Dad's mum and dad, on my own. Gateshead Place was a very short cobbled court with just seven houses in total, three on one side, four on the other. There were only three houses on one side because where the first house should have been, on the left-hand side, there stood two high wooden gates, like big doors, lying back off the roadway, enclosing a cow shed.

Of those seven houses, three contained a Jacobs family within, for as well as Nanny, Grandpa and Uncle Woolfy, living opposite them was my great-grandfather, John, Grandpa's father. This oldest living member of the Jacobs family looked just like I imagined an elderly Victorian gentleman should, resplendent in his white hair and white whiskers. I can't ever remember seeing this grand old man standing, only sitting, whether indoors on the wooden fireside armchair, or, weather permitting, outside on a chair by his front window, and always wearing big unlaced boots. Which in some ways was a bit strange as he had been a slipper maker by profession.

Great-Grandpa had first set out to meet life's challenge on 23 August 1849 by breathing in the sweet fresh air of Stoney Lane, Aldgate, where, at number 14, his mother, Rebecca, had proudly produced him for her husband, David Jacobs.

John's birth coincided with the ever-quickening pace of life in the mid-nineteenth century, with steam being employed more and more for motive power as railway lines criss-crossed the country apace and wooden sailing ships were rapidly sacrificed to iron-hulled vessels capable of holding engines strong enough to generate this new and wondrous power of navigation. What to me were old historical events I learnt about in school, such as the Crimean War, the Indian Mutiny and the American Civil War, had still not happened. Though, being a Jacobs, I've a sneaking idea that the young John would have been far more interested in the first international bare-knuckle boxing battle fought near Farnborough in 1860 between Englishman Tom Sayers and the American John C. Heenan, than in the exploits of Florence Nightingale, Robert Clive or Abraham Lincoln.

In September 1872, just before the birth of his son, my grandpa David, John moved to a small court called Providence Place in Aldgate. It is a matter of record that John and David's mother, Sarah Levey, did not get married until March 1873, though on David's birth certificate, Sarah is named as Sarah

Jacobs, nee Levey, so it is a matter of speculation whether they lived together as man and wife, which I would think they probably did as living together as an unmarried couple was not really the done thing at the time, especially amongst Jewish families.

Providence Place was hardly the most salubrious of places to live and shows yet again the poverty we Jacobses were used to as it was once described as 'a space where every kind of refuse and filth is swept, and where the water stagnates and causes the more rapid decomposition of the garbage'. In these sorts of unsanitary disease-ridden surroundings, it probably wasn't too much of a surprise when, shortly after their marriage, Sarah sadly died at the very young age of twenty-one.

Taking the plunge a second time, Great-Grandpa chose Rebecca Fox to partner him in the child-producing business, marrying her three years later. Over the next twenty years, Rebecca was to prove herself no slouch by presenting him with eleven children – Harry, Albert, Esther, Rosie, Alf, Myer, Moses, Bert, Annie, Dinah and Fred. By the time I started visiting my relatives in Gateshead Place, Rebecca had died, leaving my great-grandpa on his own – well, not exactly on his own as his house contained a ménage of Jacobses. The other occupants being his daughter Dinah, known as Dolly, and her husband Moe Levy, a small hunchbacked man; her illegitimate daughter, Rebecca; daughter Annie, unfortunately confined to a long bedlike invalid chair following an accident in her childhood and Eleazar, always called Li-Li. I was told that Li-Li was the illegitimate son of daughter, Rosie.

Dolly, despite forever washing her young daughter's hair, or so I thought through seeing this ritual taking place whenever I popped in on a Sunday, also found the time to run one of those front-room sweet shops I mentioned earlier, with a long board running along the inside of the window to hold the jars, boxes and other items of merchandise.

I have to confess that although the primary purpose of my visits to Gateshead Place on Sundays was to see Nanny and Grandpa for dinner, I always called in first at my great-grandpa's, not for any noble reason of paying court to our family's patriarch but to see my Uncle Alf. He was a tall man for those days, hovering I suppose at least around the six-foot mark, had dark brown hair and a matching coloured moustache. He was reputed to have been a bare-knuckle boxer in his younger days. He always visited his dad on Sunday morning where I, doing the very same thing by no coincidence, would meet him. A softly spoken man, he would generally ask me what I had been up to lately and that sort of small talk before finally reaching into his trouser pocket to extract the penny I had been anticipating ever since setting out for Gateshead Place that morning. To his everlasting credit I can't remember him once failing in this numismatic duty.

Uncle Alf was married to Bella and, although I never saw her to form a judgement, she was not looked upon with any great relish by Nanny and Grandpa who thought her tight-fisted and domineering, keeping the six-foot-tall ex-boxer well under her thumb.

After receiving what I had really come for, I'd bid my farewells and go across the road to have dinner with Nanny and Grandpa in their two-up, two-down, terraced house. Their front door opened on to a passage with the stairs leading up to two bedrooms about a yard to the left. To the right was the door to the front room with the back-room door some few yards further along on the same side. Passing this door, the passage ended abruptly at the scullery entrance, no door, just a wider continuation of it. Its sole contents were a gas stove, a coal- or wood-fired copper, a small wooden table and a gas pipe jutting out of the wall with a small metal tap to control the bare fishtail light it sent forth when required. On entering this haven of domesticity a door to the right opened out on to a few square yards of concrete, or, to give it its official name, the Yard, where, located along a wall to the left, exposed to all the elements, a water tap protruded with its sink below. Just past this source of sweet fresh water stood the lavatory door with the far wall covered from top to bottom in ivy just a few feet beyond it. Chickens, with their coop backing on to the ivy wall, always seemed to be pecking about on this piece of concrete, blissfully unaware that one day they would be called on to provide dinner for their owners. Though they might have been safe had it not been for the fact that Uncle Woolfy lived next door. For some reason, Grandpa was a bit squeamish about doing the deed that would bring about the chickens' demise, so he had to call on Uncle Woolfy whenever Nanny decided she wanted chicken for dinner. Uncle Woolfy seemed to have no qualms at all about wringing the poor creature's neck.

Again there was something of an ulterior motive to these visits as Nanny's Sunday dinners and afters were generally a good deal better than anything we could manage at home, especially during one of Dad's frequent periods of unemployment when our exchequer was none too healthy. They would generally be the full three-course Yiddisher *schtick*, consisting of matzo ball soup to start, a main course of either lokshen soup, salt beef, brisket or Nan's speciality, *cholent*, a delicious lamb stew, and then something like apple cake for afters.

Grandpa was a taxi driver working from the Fenchurch Street cab rank, where previously, before forsaking hay for petrol, he had driven a hansom cab. I often wondered if Sherlock Holmes had ever engaged him! Standing about 5-foot-9, slim, with greying hair and moustache, he was definitely the chief of the house, waited on hand and foot by Nan. I too held him in some awe, knowing, even at my young age, that here was a man not to be trifled with. The fact that he had been promising to buy me a nanny goat and goat cart from my earliest Gateshead Place days having nothing whatsoever to do with my keeping on his right side. The promise, alas, was never fulfilled, never honoured. I was doomed to remain goatless and goat cartless for ever. But then, when you come to think of it, where could I have kept a goat cart in the Buildings? In fact, I'm sure we would have finished up eating the goat anyway.

A prolific smoker of Player's Navy Cut cigarettes, Grandpa was a handsome contributor of their insert cards to my ever-growing collection of these small works of art.

After a while he switched his nicotine addiction to BDV, a Godfrey Phillips product, because they had advertised that, in exchange for so many tokens enclosed in their packets – God knows how many – they would endow the smoker, should he still be living, with a two-valve radio. The challenge accepted and the feat finally accomplished, Grandpa became the proud owner of his very first radio set.

How he enjoyed twiddling the knobs to try and isolate some of the words and music of the national or regional programmes from the endless hissing, spluttering and whistling it insisted on sending forth. Woe betide anyone who uttered a word during this search of the airwaves, especially if he thought he was 'on to something'.

Two regular callers on Sunday while I was visiting were the Chavra Man, from the Jewish Burial Society, to collect his weekly penny or two and Bendon, to whom a weekly amount was paid for supplying Grandpa with handmade boots. Bendon ran his boot-making business from Globe Road in Mile End. Never once did I hear his name prefixed with Mr. He was just Bendon. Grandpa's favourite boots were foot-high brown leather leggings.

In contrast to Grandpa's somewhat slender build, Nan was a big woman, a conservative estimate would be about 14 stone and 5-foot-7. Sometimes she would take me out shopping down the Lane. Always resplendent in a man's cap, she was very well known to all the stallholders who would laugh, joke and banter with her as we moved amongst them, making our purchases.

Sunday tea was no less anticipated than dinner. The main item on the menu was always Dutch herrings from Fanny Marks in the Lane and fresh watercress obtained for one penny a bunch from an itinerant vendor's barrow that had come down Gateshead Place that very same day. Just before the feast, with its accompanying bread and butter and salt and pepper, was laid out on the table, Aunt Sarah would normally appear carrying a box of pastries or a swiss roll, more often the latter.

Aunt Sarah was Nanny and Grandpa's third child, after Dad and Uncle Woolfy. She was married to Abraham Hatter, a cripple, who depended for his mobility on a pair of crutches. Thus to us he was always known as 'Abie Crutch'. How ashamed looking back can often make one feel, particularly as he was such a nice bloke.

As I said, it was Aunt Sarah who was responsible for introducing Mum and Dad to each other when she and Mum worked at Toff Levy's cigar factory. Somehow this ex-cigar maker had expanded into the tally and moneylending business and was now living a life of no little comfort in the upstairs flat of a house in Alderney Street just off Globe Road.

The only times I ever visited her house was when Mum asked me to go and see if we could borrow some money off her when we were even more hard up than usual. Once, I well remember, Mum asked me to go round and borrow five shillings from Aunt Sarah. Upon my asking this favour of her, she replied, 'Tell your mother she hasn't paid me back the last five shillings she borrowed.' She was probably right as we always seemed to be in her debt. Anyway, she gave me a good dinner and tea and when I finally left it was with two half-crowns nestling securely in my pocket. So much to us, so little to her. Having no children of her own she didn't realise I suppose the task of bringing up a large family on the poverty line.

And so, with tea out of the way, and no more food on the horizon, I bid my farewells until next week and made my way back to Sunbury Buildings ready for school in the morning.

As a postscript to the above, Great-Grandpa said goodbye to Gateshead Place and Gateshead Place said goodbye to John on a bleak January day in 1933, when he passed away in his eighty-fourth year, leaving behind him a legacy of eight sons to perpetuate the Jacobs name.

I suppose it is worth mentioning here that as a young child, Great-Grandpa would certainly have known his grandmother, Catherine Harris, who had been born in 1798 in Aldgate. She was known to be living near to him when he was born in 1849. Being fifty at the time, she could have seen him growing up a bit. The point I am making is through knowing, or even being held by, Catherine, John Jacobs would have spanned three centuries of close family ties. [To carry this on a bit further, Julie, Ikey/Alf's sister, died in 2004. She would certainly have known John Jacobs as well. So John was a linchpin, connecting family members covering four centuries – NJ.]

The following year, 1934, Gateshead Place mourned the loss of yet another Jacobs when Nanny was called to account for her sixty years at life's wicket. Her leaving the place, and so soon after his father too, left Grandpa devastated. Taken by Aunt Sarah and Uncle Abie to live with them left him like a fish out of water. His daughter's home could never replace Gateshead Place. It had no Julie. He missed her so much that it came as no great surprise to us when, in 1936, at the age of sixty-four, he went in search of her.

As for Gateshead Place itself, the small courtyard of seven two-up- two-downs just survived the war before being sacrificed to the ever-increasing demand for flats and more flats.

So as to leave no loose ends, I should also report that Uncle

Woolfy finally left and divorced Betsy, while Annie did the same to Peggy. Eventually Woolfy and Annie got married and had two further children to add to those they had with their original partners.

But the Jacobs/Joseph story didn't end there as the two names were to merge twice more when my brothers, Bill and Joe, took unto themselves, for better or for worse, Sally and Clara, two of Peggy and Annie's daughters.

And as a final footnote, when I was still visiting Gateshead Place as a boy, Nanny and Grandpa, and, indeed, Mum and Dad when talking about her at home, always referred to Annie, not as 'Becontree' Annie but as 'Black' Annie. Having never actually set eyes on her, I always assumed this was because she was rather swarthier than our family, as many of the more recent Jewish immigrants were. However, when I did eventually see her, she looked if anything whiter than us and, even more puzzling, I discovered she wasn't Jewish at all, but was of Irish extraction. It was many years before I plucked up the courage to ask Dad why she was known as 'Black' Annie. His reply was not what I expected at all. 'Why "Black" Annie?' he laughed. 'It's because her and soap are complete strangers.' I shook my head and pulled a puzzled look. So Dad added, 'She hardly ever washes.' I still showed no sign of understanding. Dad finally spelt it out, 'Her face is always dirty. That's why "Black" Annie.'

CHAPTER SEVENTEEN

THE TALLYMAN, PROVIDENT CHEQUES AND GEFILTE FISH, 1928–30

'Happy birthday, Alfie,' said Julie as she sat down to join me for breakfast. As a special treat we had bread and jam that morning. It was 21 December 1929, the day of my fourteenth birthday. The day I came of age and became a man. As it was a Saturday, there was no school that day, but, in any case, school had broken up for Christmas the day before. And, for me, reaching the ripe old age of fourteen meant no more school for me – ever! There was never ever the slightest prospect that I would stay on at school as we needed the money that I could bring in from going out to work.

Although I understood the situation only too well, I was sorry to leave Virginia Road School. I enjoyed my time there. I had made some good friends and loved learning history and

English Literature, something I was not going to have much time to be able to continue now.

Julie had already taken the plunge into the big wide world of work, having started work for Abie Goodman, a tailor in Goodman Street. Now it was my turn. Mum looked up from scraping some marge on to her bread and said, 'Make the most of the next few days, Alf, it's the last time you'll get a proper holiday.' It had been decided that as my birthday was so close to Christmas, which was the following Wednesday, there was no point in going out looking for work until Monday week, so I was allowed nine days off before looking for a job.

I had no idea what I was going to do, or even what I wanted to do, so, on the appointed day I went along to the Labour Exchange in Kingsland Road and asked them what jobs were going. They gave me a green card and sent me off to a ruling works, a small factory that manufactured lined exercise books, notebooks and notepads, in Wilson Street in Hoxton. When I arrived I asked to see the guv'nor. He came out of his office, eyed me up and down and said, 'Yes?' I showed him my green card. Without saying another word, he signed the card and handed it back to me. I wasn't sure what this meant, so I said, 'Have I got the job then?' He gave me a funny look and said, 'I've signed the card, haven't I?' There was another pause. He shook his head and tutted loudly, 'Take that back to the Labour Exchange then start work here tomorrow at eight o'clock.'

However, I didn't stick the job long. Gallons of ink were used daily to fill scores of pens from glass containers above them. But the smell of this ink gave me a continual headache. So I went back to the Labour Exchange and told them I quit my job. They weren't very happy about it but they agreed to give me another green card and sent me along to S. Finkelstein, General Woodcarver, whose place was much nearer home in Marlow Workshops. This time I knew the ropes and handed Mr Finkelstein my card. He also looked me up and down before signing the card. He seemed a bit more friendly and said, 'I know your ol' man, don't I? Jack, isn't it? He's a French-polisher.' I nodded. 'Yes, I thought so. Look, you get back here tomorrow morning and I'm sure we'll get on well together. Furniture must be in your blood.' Thinking back to my attempts at making objects in woodworking classes at school I very much doubted that, but I just nodded and said, 'Yes, Mr Finkelstein.' And with that off I skipped back to the Labour Exchange.

I now had a proper job, one I thought I could stick at. Another wage coming into the Jacobs household. With two of us children now at work, things were beginning to look up in our exchequer. However, with Dad still out of work so often and our wages being very basic, it was obvious we were still going to need a few more of my brothers to leave school and get out to work before we could live in any sort of comfort.

The family was growing up and the big problem now was clothing. Charity and second-hand could not always provide the right things at the right time, so the tallyman came on the scene. Prominent amongst this species was Blundell's, who, apart from clothing could supply anything from sheets and blankets to handkerchiefs. The way it worked was we'd choose our items from the back of their cart and then pay sixpence or one shilling per week when their representative (or tallyman as he was known) called. Mind you he had to catch us in to get the money! It was amazing just how quiet we could be when we heard his knock on the door.

One day I came home from work and I heard Mum and Dad talking about Blundell's. 'But, Jack,' Mum said, 'we can't do that.' 'We bloody well can and we bloody will,' replied Dad. Apparently what had happened was that while we were all out, Blundell's had left an unsolicited parcel of sheets and pillowcases on our doorstep. Mum had taken them in and told Dad about it when he came home. He just laughed and said, 'Keep them and when the tallyman comes to collect the money, tell him you don't know what he's talking about and that we never received any sheets or pillowcases.' Which is where I came into the conversation. 'Oh, Jack,' said Mum, 'that's dishonest, I can't lie like that.' 'Look,' Dad insisted, 'we haven't signed for anything. For all they know the parcel could have been stolen from our doorstep, so there's nothing they can do about it. Besides, it'll bloody well serve them right for pestering people with parcels they didn't ask for and getting them deeper into debt.' When the tallyman came for his money, Mum stuck to the story and Dad was right, there was nothing they could do about it, so we got some nice sheets and pillowcases free.

Provident cheques were also pressed into service. They were a better form of tally, in that they could be used for a wider range of goods in a wider range of shops. We would be issued with a cheque for, say, £1 and then pay it back at the rate of 1shilling per week for 22 weeks. These cheques were spent in shops displaying the sign, 'We take Provident cheques'. We mostly spent ours on household goods or clothes.

We used a Provident cheque to buy our first wireless. Housed in a small cabinet, it rejoiced in the trade name, 'Halcyon'. When we got into arrears and couldn't pay our weekly instalment, as happened not infrequently, the Provident collector would threaten to repossess it. At this point we would tell him it wasn't working properly and that's why we weren't paying. Naturally, he wanted proof of this, so he came in and switched it on. After a while, all that would emerge from its speaker was a vague scratchy sound. This happened several times and each time the collector agreed to let us off payment that week.

What the Provident man didn't know was that, quite by accident, we had discovered that if you rubbed a piece of wire against our fireguard while the wireless was on, it would respond with these weird noises. So, as soon as he switched on the wireless, Davy was always deputed to surreptitiously rub the fireguard.

We usually had our coal delivered on the tally system as well. There were two local coal merchants, Range and Lebon's. Range came round with his coal on the back of a cart drawn by a horse. He would arrive in the courtyard and yell out at the top of his voice, 'Coal! Coal delivery!' This could be heard all over the Buildings. However, as his coal was strictly cash on delivery, we hardly ever availed ourselves of his services. The, other merchant, Lebon's, delivered coal using a motor van, but their coal was paid for weekly, so we usually bought our coal from them. They had a very large head office on the corner of Queensbridge Road and Graham Road in Hackney.

Tarry blocks were another source of fuel. Some of the local streets were paved with wooden blocks, then tarred over. Whenever road repairs were carried out, these blocks would be taken up to be replaced by new ones. With the workmen's consent we were allowed to take the old blocks home. Mind you, even if they didn't consent, we still managed to sneak a few away.

The other main delivery we had which was paid for weekly was milk. Bellancoff, whom I had worked for briefly, was our main source of supply, but not long after I left him, he gave up his milk round and opened a small grocer shop in Virginia Road. A new milkman took over his round. He had 'Mansfield Dairies' painted on the side of his milk cart. We didn't stay with him long though because a new milkman called Ginger Jones, who had a dairy just off Columbia Road, came round soliciting business. He told Mum that his milk was 'unsurpassed for full cream'. Mum, thinking that no man would lie about so serious a subject, agreed to swap, so Ginger became our new milkman, along with his brother, who strangely had jet-black hair. At this period, the milk bottles had cardboard discs pressed into the tops for protection.

At about the time I left school we also started having bread delivered by Price's, a big well-known firm of bakers. They used handcarts and horse trolleys.

Bellancoff's new grocery shop was very handy for us as it was only about two minutes' walk away. Not long after it opened I was sent there to buy a small can of Heinz Baked Beans. This was the first time we'd ever had them, but certainly not the last as this new delicacy quickly became a favourite with the whole family – when we could afford it. Bellancoff also made his own cream cheese. Very nice with some chopped spring onion, especially in the summer.

CHAPTER EIGHTEEN

WORK, APPRENTICESHIP AND THE BOY, 1929–30

'Good morning, my boy,' said Mr Finkelstein on my first morning as I entered his workshop. 'Good morning, sir,' I replied. Although I had already had a number of part-time jobs over the last few years, I felt quite apprehensive as this time it was for real and I really needed to make it work for the good of the whole family. This could be our opportunity to crawl a little way out of the poverty trap and I knew it and it weighed quite heavily on my mind.

His workshop was situated at nos. 7 and 8 Marlow Workshops, up a flight of steep stairs. Inside I found four other men working away, none of them much older than me.

'Well, this is it,' said Mr Finkelstein, 'this is where you will be working. Ten shillings a week. Monday to Friday from eight a.m. to seven p.m. and Saturday from eight a.m. to one p.m. You get an hour for dinner and two short fifteen-minute breaks morning and afternoon.' I worked out that meant I would be working a 52-hour-week, nothing uncommon in those days, of course. In fact, the breaks seemed rather generous to me having heard what some of my old school-friends were doing.

My duties included running all the errands, getting the men's breakfasts, dinners and teas ready, sweeping up and sometimes helping with the sandpapering. If Mr Finkelstein was staying in for dinner, I had to go to Liebovitch's Kosher Restaurant in Virginia Road and pick up whatever it was he ordered. I also had to go out and get his morning coffee – milk and dash – from the ABC in Shoreditch.

The work we did in the shop came from cabinet makers who did not have enough work to justify them employing a carver of their own on the premises. My main job therefore was to go to these shops, collect the work to be done and return it when finished. Some of the cabinet makers were very fussy and always complained that something hadn't been done right. I suppose they were hoping we would give them a discount or something, but Mr Finkelstein was not a man to be messed with!

One time, not longer after I started, I had to take a carved mahogany mirror frame to a cabinet maker called Sam Phillips, whose workshop was just off Curtain Road in Hoxton, a walk of just under ten minutes. With quite a large heavy frame, it seemed a lot longer. When I arrived, I said, 'From Mr Finkelstein, your mirror.' Sam Phillips replied, 'Put it down there, boy, while I look it over.' He gave it the once over tutting all the time he was doing so. At last, he said, 'Take this back to your guv'nor, he's a butcher. Tell him I'm not paying for this rubbish. I expect better than this for what he charges.'

So off I went. Another ten-minute walk back to Marlow Workshops with this heavy frame. When I got back, I told Mr Finkelstein what Sam Phillips had said. He just nodded towards one of our benches and said to me, 'Put it under that bench.' And there it lay for three or four days untouched. Eventually, a messenger boy arrived from Sam Phillips saying that Mr Phillips wanted to know where his mirror frame was as it was holding up his work. Mr Finkelstein told him to tell his boss that it would be ready tomorrow and that it would be sent back then.

The next day, Mr Finkelstein took the frame from under the bench, wiped the dust off with his apron and said to me, 'You can take this back now.' 'But you haven't done anything to it,' I protested. 'Just take it back,' he ordered. So I did. When I presented it to Mr Phillips, he once again looked it over very closely, nodded his approval and said, 'Why didn't he do it like that in the first place?'

One of the firms I made regular visits to was Sadovsky in Ezra Street, which was just round the corner from us. The guv'nor, Simon Sadovsky, was an elderly man who ran the business with his two sons, Ronnie and Gerry. I got on well with the old man and whenever I took a particularly heavy load round, if he saw me he would give me a tip, but Gerry, who was in day-to-day charge of the business, never would. 'Put it down there,' is all I ever got from him.

Some time later, Sadovsky's moved to the Angel Furniture

Colony in Edmonton. With the pressure on to expand their businesses and the shortage of space around Shoreditch and Bethnal Green, a number of our local cabinet makers re-located there. Sadovsky's renamed themselves Beautility Furniture Co. and eventually became one of the largest furniture manufacturers in the country.

It wasn't too bad taking heavy loads a short distance as I was young and quite strong, but sometimes the load was very heavy and had to be taken some distance. On these occasions I would be sent to see Joe Levy, an upholsterer who also worked in Marlow Workshops. 'Go and ask Joe nicely if you can borrow his cart,' Mr Finkelstein would tell me, 'and don't give him any cheek.' As if I would! At first, Joe Levy was very obliging but after the first three or four times, he used to say to me things like, 'Tell your guv'nor the wheels want greasing.' Every time, I'd dutifully pass this message on to the boss, who always ignored it and said nothing. I was very puzzled by this as the wheels seemed perfectly fine to me, so I mentioned it to Archie, one of the apprentice carvers at our place, who had been 'the boy' before me. He laughed and said, 'Joe's been saying that for years. He always used to say it to me whenever I was sent to get the cart. It's his way of letting Fink know that hire of a barrow is sixpence.' I don't know if Mr Finkelstein ever paid Joe anything, but he never said no when I asked to borrow the cart.

Incidentally, Fink was the name we generally used when referring to Mr Finkelstein, at least we did when he wasn't in earshot!

Apart from Fink, Archie and me, the other three were Jack,

Alec and George Clancy. They came from all over London and some had a bit of a trek to get to work, Archie, for example, cycled in from Battersea and Alec from Peckham.

As well as being a fully qualified carver, George was also a top-class cornet player, playing solo cornet for the Haggerston Silver Band and it was a real treat for me when it was their turn to play at our bandstand as he always played the Post Horn Gallop on a post horn for an encore after playing his cornet solo. Of course, I didn't know it at the time, but George was to become a lifelong friend and work colleague until he died in 1979.

One of our best customers, a Mr Baratinsky, had his workshop in a small street off Hoxton Street up near St Leonard's Hospital, which had begun life as the Shoreditch Workhouse. Edith Cavell, that courageous nurse of the First World War, was assistant matron there from 1903 to 1906. I liked running errands there because, apart from them never having any heavy loads, Hoxton Street, with its shops and numerous stalls, I found to be very interesting and I would dawdle along looking at all the goods on display. One of the most interesting shops was Pollock's. It is still well remembered today as the shop that sold its now famous stage cut-out model sets – 'Penny plain and tuppence coloured'. Although long gone from Hoxton, a museum to its memory still exists. At one time, owned and lovingly cared for by Peter Baldwin, the actor who played Derek Wilton in Coronation Street.

To Mr Finkelstein I was always known as the 'boy'. 'Go round to Sadovsky, boy' or 'Get the dinners, boy.' At five to seven, it was 'Sweep up, boy.' After about three or four months of this boying, he said to me one day, 'Boy, tell your father I want to see him.' When I got home that night I duly told Dad what Mr Finkelstein had said. Dad tutted and said, 'What have you been up to now?' This was based on past experience as a couple of times before I had relayed a similar message and Dad was called in to hear about something I had said or done which had not pleased the guv'nor. I shrugged my shoulders as I couldn't think of anything this time.

Anyway, the following day, Dad answered the summons and Fink led him into his office, which was actually just the landing between the two doors at the top of the stairs, it being the only private place when the two doors were shut. After a while, Dad opened the door, went downstairs and left. Neither he nor Mr Finkelstein said anything to me until, at five to seven, I received the usual, 'Sweep up, boy' command.

When I got home, I was eager to know what had happened, so as soon as I got in, I said, 'Dad, what did he say? What did he say I'd done this time?' Dad who was sitting in his favourite chair, looked me up and down and, after what seemed to me to be an interminable pause, finally said, 'Mr Finkelstein wants you to be his apprentice.' I have to say that this did not come as a total surprise to me as I thought and hoped this would happen. Dad continued, 'You'll be an apprentice for five years. You won't earn much during that time but when you finish you'll have a trade in your hands and will always be able to earn a living. What do you say?' Without any hesitation, I said, 'Yes,' as it was exactly what I had wanted. My whole life and future now seemed secure and hopefully, as qualified woodcarvers were always in great demand, I would avoid the in/out work pattern that bedevilled my father and that I would be able to provide for my family much better than he had when the time came.

The next day, Dad, Mr Finkelstein and I went off to the Jewish Board of Guardians who organised apprenticeships of Jewish lads like myself and signed the necessary indentures. I was to be paid 10s. per week in the first year, 13s. the second, 17s. the third, 21s. the fourth and 25s. the fifth and final year, by which time I would be nineteen years of age.

When we got back to the workshop, Mr Finkelstein told me I would now have to get my own tools, in particular a sharpening stone and a mallet. He took me over to Parry's, a tool maker in Old Street, where together we selected the necessary items. Mr Finkelstein paid for them and told me I would have to pay him back at 1s. per week until the bill was paid, so for quite some time, my wage was just 9s. a week.

My place as the boy was not filled immediately, so, as the youngest there, I was still sent out on errands, which, to be truthful, I didn't mind as it got me out of the workshop and I was able to buy a comic, usually *The Magnet* or *The Gem*, on the way and read it before I got back. A few times, Fink remarked on the time it had taken me with some biting remark like, 'Where you been, boy? Next time take a map with you.' Or variations on this theme. Once he tried to play on my sense of responsibility by telling me how the others were relying on me doing my work properly and we were a team having to work together, a little homily he finished by saying, 'You have to remember you are no longer a boy, my boy.'

One day when I was out, Mum saw me with a sack of carvings on my back, quite a heavy one too. She stopped me and said, 'What the bloody 'ell are you doing, Alfie? You're supposed to be learning a trade not running errands.' I put the sack down to talk to her and she went to pick it up. 'Bleedin' 'ell, Alf, that's bloody heavy. You wait till your father hears about this. Sam Whatsisname won't know what's hit him.' Worrying that my little comic-reading scam could be in jeopardy here, I pleaded with Mum not to say anything. I said, 'We're stuck at the moment, Mum, Mr Finkelstein is trying to get a replacement for me but we haven't got one yet, so I'm just helping out. Once we get a new boy, I'll be on the bench full time.' Mum didn't look very pacified and sure enough that night, when Dad came home, she duly reported what she had witnessed with her very own eyes.

The next day, Dad and Mr Finkelstein had another meeting in his office. Once again, Dad left without either of them saying a word to me. It was about an hour later when Fink came over to me and said, 'I am trying to get another boy, you know.' I nodded and said I was sorry and that I had tried to explain the position to Mum and Dad.

That evening, Dad said, 'I told your guv'nor you're not to run any more errands, you're there to learn a trade, not break your back carrying heavy sacks.' I just nodded.

As it happens, Mum and Dad's intervention didn't make much difference and I still ran a few errands, though I kept a look-out for Mum while I was running them. Someone had to do it as our livelihood depended on the work coming in and going out in good time.

However, about two weeks after this incident, a new boy, Henry Ross, took my place and I wasn't asked to run any more errands or sweep the floor or get the dinners. And to prove I had now moved up the ladder, Mr Finkelstein called me into his office and told me that from now on he would call me Alf and I could call him Sam.

CHAPTER NINETEEN

OPERA, BODYLINE AND BEANOS, 1929–36

'I'm on the bench now, you know. I'm a proper woodcarver and this is our new errand boy, Henry.'

As the ex-boy, one of my first duties was to take Henry out and introduce him to all our customers which I did with those words. Of course, all our customers knew I had only just started as an apprentice and wasn't a proper woodcarver, but it gave me a great sense of pride and authority to be able to say I was and to be able to introduce someone junior to me. None of them burst my bubble and all nodded, some even saying things like, 'Well done, Alf, so you've made it now.' I beamed with satisfaction and delight that they should recognise me in this way.

Henry wasn't a bad sort at all. He was only a few months younger than me and his father worked for Zinkins, a big furniture manufacturer in Mare Street, Hackney, and also ran a newspaper stand on Sunday mornings on the corner of Middlesex Street and Bishopsgate, where Henry earned a bob or two by helping out. We got on well together and even went on the odd night out together, either to the pictures or just for a stroll up West. He lived with his parents and younger sister near the Children's Hospital just off Hackney Road.

'I'm packing in this woodcarving lark, Alf,' Alec said to me one morning a few months later. 'I don't think it's really me.' In truth I wasn't that shocked as, from what I saw of his work, he didn't really have the aptitude and made a lot of mistakes. Nevertheless, he was a likeable chap, so I said, 'Oh, I'm sorry to hear that, Alec. What will you do?'

'I've got an office job,' he replied. 'My dad works at the Foreign Office and he knows someone who was looking for help in his office.' 'Sounds a bit boring to me, Alec,' I said, 'still, if it's what you want to do, good on you.'

So Alec became the first to leave Sam's while I was there. He was followed shortly afterwards by George Clancy, who decided to start up in business for himself. He rented a very old and dilapidated shop in Hare Street, just off Brick Lane, later moving to Streatley Workshops in the Buildings, where he remained until his King and Country beckoned in 1939. Many times during my apprenticeship, he would ask me to help him out. As this happened mostly during the busy periods leading up to Christmas and Easter, I would quite likely be doing one or two hours overtime at Sam's already, so I would work from 7 a.m. to 8 p.m. there, go home for a bite to eat and then go round to George to work from about 8.30 to 10 or 11 p.m. All the work I did for George was paid on piecework, so the more I did the more I earned. When things were very busy, it was not unusual to work until 5 p.m. on Saturdays and sometimes even Sunday mornings.

Sam was obliged to pay us well above apprenticeship rates for overtime, otherwise it would not have been worth doing, so the agreement was 6d. per hour for the first year, rising by 3d. per hour each year until it reached 1s.6d. by the final year. At times like this when I was working overtime and working flat out for George I was able to contribute a fair wedge to the Jacobs coffers, easing our situation and allowing us to buy whole eggs and fresh bread amongst other luxuries.

Sam did not replace Alec and George, relying instead on taking on part-time employees during the busy periods and laying them off when things slackened off a bit. During the quieter periods, it was hard for Sam to get his bills settled on time. Sam Phillips and Sadovsky were good payers, but it was always very much in the lap of the gods how much money he would get in from the others. The majority of our customers depended on selling the furniture they had made that week to pay their own workers. If they couldn't sell much, or even in some cases, any at all, the woodcarver came low down on their list of priorities and sometimes Sam was lucky if he even got half of what he was owed.

Jack was appointed to be my mentor and to teach me the ropes and help me become a properly qualified woodcarver. Until he became my mentor I only knew him as Jack, so I asked him what his full name was, 'John, John Gilbert,' he replied. I laughed and Jack gave me a funny look. 'What's so funny?' he asked. 'No, what's your real name?' I said. 'I've just told you.' I looked at him more in puzzlement than anything else now. 'No,' I said, 'you're pulling my leg. John Gilbert?' 'What's wrong with that?' he said, starting to look a little annoyed. 'But John Gilbert's a big film star,' I said, 'he's a friend of Greta Garbo's.' Jack just shook his head and tutted. 'Is that really your name?' I continued, a little more defensively. 'Yes, you *putz*, it really is my name,' he replied.

In spite of this somewhat awkward beginning, a friendship sprang up between us, although there were some three years between our ages. He was an orphan who had spent his early years in the Jewish Orphanage in Norwood. When he started work for Sam, he found lodgings in Stoke Newington with a Mr and Mrs Magnus, who treated him more as an adopted son than a lodger.

I used to visit him after work on Saturdays and sometimes on Sundays. To my amazement he had his own room, a luxury I had never enjoyed and, even better, he had a radiogram all to himself. It was in this room that a new dimension to my life began – opera! Jack loved opera and very soon so did I. He never had complete albums of these works but what he had were records of well-known singers singing popular arias. Amongst the great voices we listened to were Tom Burke, John McCormack and Jan Kiepura. but my absolute favourite was Alfred Piccaver singing 'Song of Songs'. This man went on to become a legend in his own lifetime. He went to Austria to sing with the Vienna State Opera for over twenty years. When he died in the 1950s, all Vienna turned out for his funeral – well, nearly all. He was a small rotund man, but, boy, he sure had some voice!

The next step for me now was to go and see the real thing, a complete opera on stage. So, accompanied by Jack, I paid my first visit to Sadler's Wells. As luck would have it, I saw two for the price of one because they were doing what we cognoscenti called Cav and Pag, or to those not in the know as I was then, *Cavalleria Rusticana* and *I Pagliacci*. To put it mildly, I was spellbound by the sheer beauty of it all. The Easter Hymn from *Cavalleria Rusticana* welling up from that stage and enveloping us all in its magic was something I will never forget. In my life I have heard many famous people sing the lead roles in these two operas but that night's stars, Arthur Cox as Canio and Percy Manchester as Turiddu, are the ones I always remember.

Of the other operas we saw, *The Marriage of Figaro* was my favourite and endeared Mozart to me from that day to this. The first time I saw it, the lead roles were admirably handled by those two long-running favourites at the Wells, Joan Cross and Sumner Austin.

As well as opera I was also interested in other forms of culture and one day I thought it would be a good idea to visit the British Museum. I'm not sure what I was expecting exactly, but I'd heard they had lots of Egyptian mummies there and, as I had never seen an Egyptian mummy before, I thought this might add to my general quest for a bit of learning.

So one Saturday morning as we were all having breakfast, I announced my intention of visiting the British Museum that day. As I was due to go into work in the morning, I asked Mum if she could have some sandwiches ready for me at lunchtime so I could just nip home for a quick visit after work and then go up to the Museum taking my lunch with me.

When I returned home, Mum gave me my sandwiches and said, 'You make sure you look after the other boys, Alfie.'

'What other boys?' I asked, not sure what she meant.

'After you left this morning, Davy, Bill, Abie and Joey said they'd like to go with you.'

I hadn't expected this at all. I thought I would be able to get away on my own for the afternoon, but the others were all picking their packed lunches up off the table looking very excited at the prospect of this visit up West to such a famous place. 'OK, then,' I said, knowing there was no point in arguing. 'Let's go.'

As we shut the door to the flat, our next-door neighbour, Aaron Da Costa, happened to be coming out of his door. Seeing us all clutching our sandwiches wrapped up in some old newspaper, he said, 'Are you going somewhere?' 'Yes,' I replied, we're all going up to the British Museum to see the mummies.' 'Can I come?' he asked. 'No, I don't think so,' I replied. It was bad enough being responsible for all my brothers, I didn't want this additional responsibility as well. Aaron looked a bit crestfallen as we all set off down the stairs.

As we walked out of the gate to the Buildings, Aaron came running up behind us. 'Are you sure I can't go?' he asked again. 'No,' said Abie, 'now go away, Aaron.' As we made for Navarre Street, Aaron continued to follow us. We kept looking round but he was still there as we strode into Boundary Street. Eventually, Abie turned round and shouted at him, 'I told you to go away, Aaron, we don't want you with us. This is for the Jacobs boys only.' Aaron hesitated slightly and we moved on. On reaching Redchurch Street, he caught up with us again and said, 'Look, I've come all this way already, can't I go with you?' 'Just fuck off, Aaron,' came Abie's curt reply. But Aaron didn't fuck off, instead he continued to follow and every now and then would catch us up to ask if he could go with us.

We were all feeling pretty fed up with this and felt he was spoiling our day out and again it was Abie who finally snapped. As we reached Bethnal Green Road, there was a fish shop on the corner, so Abie turned round to Aaron and said, 'Look we've told you, you can't come with.' And with that, he picked Aaron up bodily and dumped him in a barrel of Dutch herrings that stood on the pavement outside the shop.

Aaron didn't bother us again after that and we continued to have a pleasant day out at the British Museum, where I at last got to see my first mummies. In spite of the irritation caused by Aaron, I have to say the experience was well worth it and I was truly awestruck by what I saw, and visited the British Museum as often as I could after, looking at the different exhibits.

As well as 'culture', my other great leisure activity was sport. I was an avid reader of the newspaper sports pages. Cricket was the national game then and I knew nearly every player in the County Championship and which team they played for. My favourite county was Surrey, with the incomparable Percy Fender as captain, and I followed their fortunes religiously.

In those days, Test matches, especially the Ashes series against the eternal enemy, Australia, dominated the newspapers and wireless. I well remember the furore caused by bodyline bowling in the 1932–33 series out in Australia. Bodyline was a tactic devised by the England captain, Douglas Jardine, together with his two fast bowlers, Harold Larwood and Bill Voce, where the cricket ball was bowled at the body of the batsman in the hope that, when he defended himself with his bat, a resulting deflection could be caught by one of several fielders standing close by. It was devised by the English cricket team specifically to combat the extraordinary batting skill of Australia's greatest ever batsman, Don Bradman. Australia considered this to be intimidatory and physically threatening, to the point of being unfair in a game that was supposed to uphold gentlemanly traditions. Public reaction in both England and Australia was outrage directed at the other nation. Towards England for the tactic itself and towards Australia for accusing England of being ungentlemanly. The row escalated to the highest levels with both countries' governments threatening to boycott trade with the other. It was eventually settled with Australia apologising to England and the MCC introducing new laws to try and prevent bodyline bowling.

My own view was that Jardine had the right idea. He put those Aussies in their place despite some of his own people, especially one of his other fast bowlers, Gubby Allen, turning on him. I wonder what Jardine's critics would think of fast bowling in cricket these days!

My first venture away from the newspapers to the real thing was to see Essex play at Leyton, where they used to play two county matches every year.

Football soon became another passion and visits to Highbury to see Arsenal followed soon after. This was the period of their heyday under Herbert Chapman, when they were easily the best club in England, winning numerous league and cup titles. The team featured many England internationals, including the

England captain, Eddie Hapgood, as well as the likes of Alex James and Cliff Bastin.

I often went to football with my mates from the Buildings, usually the football-mad Ginger Roplitt, but most of them weren't so keen on cricket so there were often times when I made the pilgrimage to Leyton on my own.

Boxing and wrestling also gained my attention. Most matches were held in the evenings on weekdays or the afternoon at weekends. Bethnal Green Drill Hall had a large open space at the rear where they pitched the boxing ring in the summer.

One day we all flocked down there to see Archie Sexton, a great local favourite and British Middleweight title contender, take on an unknown Aussie called Wally Hancock, who, rumour had it, had only arrived in England by boat that very day. A piece of cake for our man, we all thought. The MC made the customary introductions, after which the gladiators went to their respective corners. A great hush fell over the arena and the bell clanged to mark the start of what we hoped would be an absorbing contest. Immediately, Hancock tore across the ring and, with one punch, knocked Archie Sexton out. The fight was all over in seconds.

I never heard any more of Wally Hancock after that memorable evening. As for Archie, he did go on to fight for the British Middleweight title but lost in the tenth round to Jock McAvoy. Perhaps his greatest claim to fame though was that he was the father of Dave Sexton, later Chelsea and Manchester United football manager.

Towards the mid-thirties, Jack Solomons, a local fishmonger, started promoting boxing at the Devonshire Hall in Hackney.

It was here that I first set eyes on Eric Boon, popularly known as Boy Boon, who was later to become British Lightweight champion. His fight with Alf Danahar at the Albert Hall was talked about in Bethnal Green for many years afterwards.

The most famous boxer of the period, especially to us young Jewish kids, was Kid Berg, a local Jewish lad just like us, born in Stepney. He went on to become not just the British lightweight champion but also World champion.

There were a number of good local boys boxing, amongst them my old friend and neighbour, Jackie Da Costa, who fought under the ring name of Johnnie Cunningham. Another was Dickie Corbett, who later tragically lost his life in the staircase disaster at Bethnal Green Station during the war.

All-in wrestling was then, as it still is today, dominated by the goodies and the baddies. The three Pye Brothers, Jack, Harry and Bully, were the meanest wrestlers around. But to us Jews, the most hated fighter was Karl Reginsky. The posters stuck up round the neighbourhood whenever he was due to wrestle proclaimed him to be a 'Thoroughbred German Nazi'. Invariably he would be matched with a Jewish wrestler, whom he would beat handsomely. Of course, it was all the promoter's gimmick, of which I was quite unaware at the time. When I got a bit older and wiser I discovered that Reginsky was himself a Jew. However, the huge Jewish following who went to all his bouts, hoping and praying for his demise, must have made him much richer than the average wrestler.

I took a great interest in other sports as well, including lawn tennis. Did we not have the two greatest players in the world at this time in Fred Perry and Dorothy Round, both Wimbledon Champions?

Speedway, with such stalwarts as Jack Parker, Tiger Stevenson and Eric Langton among the best in the world all doing battle for England against the arch enemy from Down Under, who themselves boasted stars such as Max Grosskreutz, Vic Huxley and Bluey Wilkinson. These were great days for speedway, then still in its infancy and arguably at the peak of its popularity.

Though I was interested enough to follow the sport in the newspapers I wasn't as mad keen as Abie and Joey, who, with their friend Joly Parker, used to go and see it live one or more times a week. In London during the 1930s, there was a meeting on somewhere every night of the week, except Sunday, and there were a number of occasions when Abie and Joey went to six meetings a week.

As far as horse racing was concerned, the Derby and the Grand National were national events and had people talking and arguing about the merits of the various entries with their jockeys and trainers weeks before the events took place. The street bookmakers reaped a rich harvest from these self-proclaimed knowledgeable followers

Billiards and snooker, with the acknowledged masters of these two indoor sports – such as Joe Davis, Tom Newman and Willy Smith along with the Australian wizard, Walter Lindrum – were very popular at the time. Funnily enough, given how popular snooker has now become thanks mainly to television, it was billiards that was by far the more popular of the two in the 1930s. All the big matches were held at Thurston's or Burroughs and Watts in the West End of London.

Athletics with Sidney Wooderson and Jack Lovelock and golf with Abe Mitchell, Alf Padgham and Henry Cotton were two more sports I kept my eye on through the newspapers.

But, cricket and football apart, the biggest sporting event in the country, the event that held everybody's attention, was the Boat Race. Weeks before it took place, the papers would keep us informed of the time trials of each crew along with photos of the rowers involved. Children would wear the favours of the University they 'voted for' and, as the great day drew near, the excitement mounted. And when the day finally did arrive, nearly all the newspapers would devote their entire front page to the monumental struggle ahead, with latest news of the crews, the positions each man would take up in the boat and their prediction for the winner.

By the time of the boats' departure from Putney, practically the whole nation would be gathered round their wirelesses to follow the fortunes of their favourite university, with the commentators doing their best to make the race sound interesting, not an easy task when one boat took a lead early on and went miles ahead. After the race was over, it was not unusual to see kids who had previously been sporting the losers' favour, suddenly be seen wearing that of the victors. After all, predicting the winner of the Boat Race was a very serious business and nobody wanted to be on the losing side.

As I grew older I would sometimes go for a night out with Dad after work, to his club, where I became quite a good darts player and was invited to join the Metropolitan Club team. I tried my hand at billiards and snooker but was pretty hopeless at both. Dad was the club's best player and I threatened his position not one iota. Though I did have the satisfaction of being a little bit better than my brother, Davy, who it was generally reckoned was the worst billiards player around. Sometimes as you entered the club a billiard ball might come bouncing down the stairs. The common cry on seeing this happen was, 'I see Davy's in tonight.'

On Sunday mornings I would meet up with four or five mates my age from the Buildings and we'd go along to one of the local pubs, either the Birdcage, the Three Loggerheads or the Conqueror.

It was through the Conqueror that I renewed my acquaintance with the seaside after a period of some five years since my trip to Weymouth. This time it was a beano that brought me back to the sea one Sunday in August. The morning was bright and sunny, and, armed with plenty of booze, sandwiches, hardboiled eggs and bread and butter, we left Bethnal Green for that pearl of East Coast resorts, Southend-on-Sea. Halfway along the Arterial Road, the charabanc stopped, unloaded the beer and eats and there, in the clean countryside, we refreshed ourselves. Refreshment stop over, the leftovers were packed aboard and practically everyone disappeared into the woods to lighten their load. Once aboard again we headed non-stop for Southend.

On arriving, we were given a time and place (Lockhart's) to report to for high tea and then we were free to do as we pleased. Most made for the local pubs, but a few of us, who weren't really heavy drinkers, gave the town, pier and Kursaal a good looking-into.

On the way home, we stopped at the Halfway House in

Laindon for about an hour for yet more booze. On the final leg of the journey home, my voice blended in perfectly with the others, even though I had hardly touched any beer.

Beanos were a way of life in those days. Nearly all pubs and clubs had them, even factories. A few coppers a week ensured a good day out in the summer for working-class people. I suppose its equivalent today would be a holiday on one of the Costas.

After a while, we made the Three Loggerheads, run by Jack Stuart, our main port of call. I joined their darts team and played for them every Wednesday night, one week at home, the next away. Two of my mates, Teddy Payne and Percy Bates, also joined the team. Percy was also an old classmate of mine, who, like me, had been very interested in history. However, it is sad to think that since leaving school, nobody has ever asked me about the Earl of Leicester, Horace Walpole or Pitt the Older, not even the Younger. A good education wasted!

Now, Percy, who lived in Streatley Buildings, had a sister named Sophie. She was about a year younger than me. Of course, I had known her for many years, but suddenly we found we were no longer children but young adults, so I thought it must be my duty to fall in love with her because in lots of films I had seen this was the normal course of events with friends forever falling in love with their friend's sister. It was expected. She may have seen the same films because one day when I met her in the Loggerheads with her brother, I took her to one side and asked her if she'd like to come to the pictures with me and she immediately said, 'Yes.' So we went and we went out a few more times, but I discovered this love thing wasn't all it was cracked up to be and I had no particular feelings for Sophie. To me, she was still Percy's younger sister.

To complicate matters even more I started to get pally with a girl in the Loggerheads called Philippa, who was a good darts player, so we teamed up and together we won the Watney's Area Darts Championship. The prize for this was a trophy and a gold enamelled medal each.

Our relationship grew a little deeper than just darts, and unbeknown to Sophie I took Philippa out to the pictures a couple of times where we sat in the back row holding hands, amongst other things, something I never felt any inclination to do with Sophie. So I already felt a bit of a cad for double-timing her. But now things got even more complicated as Philippa asked me if she could have my medal to go with hers as a keepsake and to show our affection for each other. This was a real problem for me as I had been offered 5 shillings for my medal, a not inconsiderable sum of money, so I made some feeble excuse for not parting with it and sold it a little while later. I now felt like a double unmitigated cad though we still carried on seeing each other.

But things were to get even worse as Philippa's mother contracted meningitis and died soon afterwards. We were all shocked as she was such a nice person. Following the death of his wife, Philippa's father decided to leave their house and move to Whetstone in Hertfordshire, taking Philippa with him. With her now living so far away it became impossible to carry on our relationship and we decided we had no option but to call it a day. I was miserable and oh, how I wished I'd given her my medal. In addition to that, at about the same time, Sophie said to me, 'I don't think this is working, do you, Alf?' I had to agree and that was the end of that relationship as well.

CHAPTER TWENTY

HAMPSTEAD HEATH, LORD BOND STREET AND THE CHESTERFIELD, 1931–6

'Mrs Jacobs?' the man asked when Mum opened the door.

'Yes,' she replied a bit warily, wondering what this stranger could possibly want with her.

'Did your boy, David, start work at the sawmill today?'

Mum was even more wary, 'Why do you want to know?' she asked.

'Well, he's just been taken to St Leonard's Hospital.'

'What!?' Mum screamed. 'Why? What's happened? Is he all right?'

'He had a nosebleed at work,' the man said calmly. This seemed to reassure Mum a bit and she calmed down. 'Oh, yes,' she said, 'he's always having nosebleeds.'

It was true, Davy and Dad suffered a lot from nosebleeds and could often be seen at home laid out on the floor with cold keys placed at the back of their necks, which was thought to be the cure for this condition.

Mum continued, 'There's really no need to take him to the hospital.'

The man nodded. 'Er . . . this was a bit different to an ordinary nosebleed. A piece of wood shot out of a planing machine and struck him on the nose.'

As it happened, Dad was at home (out of work, of course) and overheard much of the conversation. He came to the door and said, 'What sort of bloody sawmill are you running there? It's Davy's first day and you let this happen to him.'

'I can assure you, it was an accident, Mr Jacobs,' the man replied.

'I should bloody well hope it was,' said Dad, not really reassured. 'I mean, you'd hardly do it on purpose, would you?' Then turning to Mum, he said, 'Get my coat, Becky, I'm off down the hospital.'

Davy eventually spent two nights at the hospital before having his nose cauterised and being sent home.

Apart from his regular nosebleeds, this was not the first time Davy had had an incident involving a lot of blood. When he was nine years old he had decided to hitch a lift on the back of an open lorry, as many of us boys did at that time. However, he fell off into the road and was run over by a horse and cart that was close behind. This happened in Bethnal Green Road. He managed to struggle home where Mum removed his blood-soaked jacket and put him in bed. Our panel doctor, Dr Vivian Ridewood, was called out to see him and he proclaimed that

Davy had broken both his legs. He recommended he stay in bed until they mended. Dr Ridewood visited every few days to see how the patient was doing and after about six or eight weeks it was decided his legs had healed and he could go back to school. But his legs remained a bit of a funny shape for ever after and he had a bit of a stiff gait and was unable to move quickly or run properly. Maybe if they had put his legs in plaster or put splints on them it might all have turned out differently. But what do I know? I'm not a doctor.

Dad forbade Davy to return to the sawmill, so his first job lasted just one day, less time than even I had done at the inking works. A couple of days later, Uncle Woolfy came round to visit us and Dad regaled him with Davy's story of the sawmill.

'So, are you looking for a job now, Davy?' Uncle Woolfy asked. Davy nodded. 'Well, I think I have just the thing for you. As you know, I started work at Eldorado [a big ice-cream company] a couple of months ago and they're looking for a salesman. With your gift of the gab you'd be ideal for the job.' Davy liked the sound of this and said, 'Thank you, Uncle Woolfy, yes, I'll have a go.'

'It pays well and there's good commission,' Uncle Woolfy continued. 'I'll have a word tomorrow and let you know.'

Good as his word, Uncle Woolfy did speak to someone and fixed Davy up with a job. Not only did he now have a job but it was to be instrumental in deciding Davy's future in one other very important way, as whilst selling ice cream to the Astoria Cinema in New Cross one afternoon about two years later, he noticed a very good-looking young lady usherette with the most beautiful blonde hair. Not being the shy sort,

Davy went straight up to her and said, 'Hello, what's your name? I'm Davy.'

The usherette looked him up and down and finally replied, 'I'm Connie.'

'OK, Connie,' Davy continued, 'what time do you get off later?' And this was the start of a romance that was later to lead to marriage and four children.

Bill was the next of my brothers to greet the cruel hard world of work. He tried his hand at a furrier in Bishopsgate but had to pack it in because of his poor eyesight. He eventually went on to become a French-polisher like Dad.

Incidentally, Davy also eventually became a French-polisher after leaving the delights of the ice-cream world. It was said that he became a real master craftsman. There was even one occasion, when he was very delicately colouring in the grain on a repair, that he took the ever-present roll-up out of his mouth so as not to drop fag-ash on the work, so dedicated was he to his art.

As the youngest, Manny, was still at school, Mum and Dad thought it would be a good idea to teach him how to play the piano. They could both play, though neither could read music, so they thought it would be good idea if Manny learnt to play properly, music and all. With four extra wages now coming into the household, they were just about able to buy a piano on hire purchase from a music shop called Parker's in Bishopsgate. It then had to be manhandled up eight flights of stairs to the flat as there were no lifts in those days. A music teacher called Alf Harris, who played the piano at Dad's favourite club, the Metropolitan, was engaged to come up once a week to teach Manny.

About six months later, the piano had to be manhandled all the way down again because the council, in its wisdom, had decided that, as there were so many adults in the flat, it now came under the heading of 'overcrowded'. They therefore allocated us a three-bedroom flat on the ground floor in nearby Sonning Buildings. So you could say we were coming down in the world, but in this case, that was a good thing.

With four children working and a ground-floor flat, life was decidedly better for us. We still had to get our water from the landing outside and had to go out there for our lavatory, but, at least it was our own and not a shared sink and toilet.

As well as the extra income from us kids, Dad thought up another money-making scheme. A stall at Hampstead Heath Fair, which operated on Easter Monday, Whit Monday and August Bank Holiday Monday. The fair was very popular with many families out for a good time and prepared to part with their cash. The stall was called 'Cover The Red Spot' and was purely and simply a game of skill. A red circle had to be covered completely by five smaller flat metal discs. There was only one correct method of laying the discs. The only stipulation was that once laid, the disc couldn't be moved, otherwise people could have been there all day moving the discs around until they hit on the right combination.

I was taken along on these occasions to help Dad out. My job was to casually pass by every half an hour or so, while Dad called out to me, 'Oi, sonny, you look like a clever boy. Come and see if you can do it.' Of course I knew the secret and did it in double quick time. Seeing that a young boy could do it so easily soon had members of the public queueing up with their sixpence a time to have a go. Behind the stall was a backcloth on which hung about half a dozen watches. One of these was the glittering prize awaiting anyone who could perform the task successfully. As far as I knew, not one of the watches was in working order, but as nobody ever won one, a small thing like that didn't really matter.

I used to enjoy the long journey on the Tube from Old Street to Hampstead, the deepest station on the Underground. Over the few years I helped out I became very well known to the showmen. Sometimes one of them would call upon me to mind his stall while he slipped away on 'urgent business', aka a pint in the local hostelry. So a bit more cash to add to the finances.

It was only three times a year but it certainly boosted our exchequer substantially on those days.

So just as we seemed to be reaching what to us was a reasonably good comfortable life there was a slight setback to the ever-improving financial situation when one Sunday morning Mum called us all together after breakfast and announced, 'I've got some good news for you all. You'll soon be having a new baby brother or sister to play with.' Exactly ten years to the day after Manny was born, there was another addition to our family when Mum at the ripe old age of forty-five gave birth to a baby girl, Clara. The ground-floor flat was worth its weight in gold as our heavily pregnant Mum would have found it very difficult traipsing up and down eight flights of stairs each day and then having to carry the pram up and down.

Moving into a new flat meant we had a new set of neighbours to get used to. Next door to us was a husband, wife and three boys, called Buller. There was another man in Sonning – I was never sure where he lived exactly – called Campbell who used to offer a toffee ball to anyone who would fight Buller. I can only assume that at some point in the past, Mr Campbell was wronged by Mr Buller, but nothing ever came of this offer.

Opposite us on our landing was a man we knew as 'Chick'. He lived there with his sixteen-year-old daughter. One day he arrived home with a brand-new wireless. It had no batteries or accumulator, you just plugged it in the wall and away it went. Amazing! He was so proud of this wonder of modern technology that he would leave his door open so that everyone else on the landing could share in his joy. To reward him for this unselfish action, we tried out our old Sunbury trick of rubbing a piece of wire along the fireguard. It worked a treat, leaving Chick a puzzled and very worried man. After that he played it behind closed doors, leaving us in peace, although we did perhaps give a little rub every now and then just in case he ever thought of opening his door again.

Next to him, at number 22 lived Arthur Lee. Now he was something else. He had a wife, two daughters, Flossie and Connie, and a newly born baby boy, for whom Arthur had already mapped out a career as a surgical instrument maker. We never knew why that particular career; perhaps it sounded important to Arthur.

Arthur was a small man and worked as a van driver for Eva and Son, Haulage Contractors. If I had nothing to do, he would take me for a ride in his van to wherever he was going. But what made Arthur stand out as a character amongst characters was his burning desire to own Bond Street, which he really believed was his by right.

The maiden name of Arthur's grandmother on his mother's side was Bond and, over years of visiting various record offices and combing through their archives, he became convinced she had something to do with Bond Street, her family at one time owning it. Arthur made it his mission in life to restore that illustrious street to its rightful owner, namely himself. He would write off to all sorts of people and places in pursuit of any intelligence that might help to put right this dreadful wrong done to him and to reclaim his birthright.

Many's the day I would try to help him decipher rolls and sheets of paper with family trees while Arthur was reading and making notes, footnotes, headnotes or any other sort of note he thought relevant to his cause. Every time I helped him he would promise me with great sincerity that I would not be forgotten when this great injustice was finally put right. Arthur was a man obsessed.

Now it so happened that Arthur's wife thought he was a complete nutter. Mind you to her everlasting credit she never tried to burst his bubble and kept her own opinion of his quest to herself. But when I spoke to her about it, I gathered that was her view of his desire to become Lord Bond Street.

Was Arthur chasing rainbows or was there really a crock of gold just out of his reach? Who knows? Sadly, he died unlorded and relatively poor after being rehoused on the Debden Estate in Loughton after the war.

Milly Murphy lived in the next block to us. She was a widow with four children. A more pleasant and likeable person it would be difficult ever to come by. She used to arrive home from work in the evening singing the song that was known to all of us in the Buildings as Milly's Song. To everyone else, it was called 'Danny Boy'. Tragically she lost three of her children shortly after we moved in. Eileen, a lovely sixteen-year-old girl, Tommy, who was about fourteen, and Young Nobby who was just six years old. I never knew what they died of but it was all very sad. Only her eldest daughter, also called Milly, lived on. A further tragedy was to strike the family during the war when the mother was killed during a bomb raid on Bethnal Green.

Charlie and Katie Carter lived just across the yard. They were quite pally with Mum and Dad and had two children, both boys. Charlie was by trade a fowl plucker and worked in Petticoat Lane market. I once saw him at work and I was amazed at the speed he and his colleagues were able to strip a chicken of all its plumage. To us at home it was a laborious task, the only real downside to having a nice bowl of lokshen soup.

One day Charlie was involved in an accident at work and was rushed to hospital. The outcome of this was that he had to have a testicle removed, something which caused much merriment and joking amongst the neighbours, including us, I am ashamed to say. However, Charlie had the last laugh. With the money he received in compensation he hired a taxi to take him and his family out for the day to Margate, something unheard of for working-class people.

Two floors above us, there lived the Fairmans, Peter and Ada, with their two daughters, Betsy and Ginny, as well as a grandson, known to one and all simply as 'Boyboy'. Peter was very small, while Ada was a very large woman, a typical Donald McGill seaside postcard couple. Except that Peter was not in the least henpecked. He was the acknowledged ruler of the castle.

Betsy seemed to be carrying on a very strange affair. She was in her mid-thirties and was being courted by Will, a man who must have been between fifty-five and sixty. Will worked for a travelling showman at various fairgrounds around the country, so the courtship was far from continuous. Will would turn up half a dozen or so times a year, stay a few days and then be off on his travels again. As far as I know they never married. I don't think anybody expected them to – except perhaps Betsy.

Betsy's second great love after Will was a new Chesterfield sofa she bought second-hand, very second-hand! Although not in the best of nick, it became the apple of her eye while Will was away. After all, a working-class girl with such a luxurious piece of furniture was virtually unheard of. Now it might have been that she had her swain in mind when acquiring this handsome commodity, somewhere they could cuddle up and maybe more when the rest of the household were out, but from the moment it was installed, all the block, nay, all the Buildings knew about it. She would go downstairs to the yard a good half a dozen times a day and call up to her sister, 'Ginny, can you bring me down my handbag please, I think I left it on the Chesterfield.' Or 'Ginny, can you bring down my handkerchief, I think I left it on the Chesterfield.' The word Chesterfield would be emphasised in a very loud voice so that no one anywhere in the Buildings could be in any doubt where Betsy had left the article in question, nor miss the fact that she owned a Chesterfield. Also, when speaking to her anywhere inside or outside the Buildings, she would contrive to bring her beloved Chesterfield into the conversation somehow or other. It was to her what Bond Street was to Arthur Lee. The one big exception, of course, being that she did actually own the Chesterfield. It became such a joke to us that whenever anyone lost anything in our flat, someone else would be sure to say, 'Have you looked on the Chesterfield?'

'Boyboy' was about twelve or thirteen years of age and regarded as a bit simple. He was well liked and a bit of a character (but then who wasn't in our Buildings!); he once told us that somebody had put a live jellied eel down his back. He had been given a pair of wellingtons, by the look of them probably made during the great man's lifetime. He thought they were wonderful. A Chesterfield and a pair of wellingtons in one family, it was unbelievable. Whenever it rained, Boyboy would be seen standing in the middle of the playground, with no hat or coat on, beaming down at his wellies. His feet must have got soaking wet on these occasions but it was a small enough price to pay for being the owner of such renowned footwear.

Ginny was a very introverted girl, aged between about eighteen and twenty I should think. Her main function in life seemed to be to search for the various articles left by Betsy on the Chesterfield.

The whole block knew when Peter came home from work because, as soon as he entered the block, he would cry out in a very loud voice, 'Ada Gockle! Ada Gockle!' and would continuing shouting all the way up the stairs until he got indoors.

CHAPTER TWENTY-ONE

THE WOODEN TOE AND LAW BREAKING, 1935–6

'Alfie, have you seen Manny anywhere on your way home?' Mum asked me one evening just as I arrived back from work in time to see everyone else tucking into their fried-fish dinner.

'No,' I replied.

Mum looked a bit worried, 'He went out ages ago just after school and should be home by now for his tea.'

Of course, as kids we spent a lot of time outside and normally it wouldn't be too much to worry about, but he had been gone a long time and everyone was expected to be back for teatime.

'Don't worry,' I said. 'I expect he'll be back soon.'

'Yes, I guess you're right, Alfie. I'll just have to get used to the idea that Manny is no longer the baby and he's growing up fast.'

The arrival of Clara had changed what had become a fairly ordered life for us and things were never quite the same again after her arrival. I have to admit it was very strange having a baby in our midst again after all this time. How Mum managed to cater for nine grown-ups and a baby, I'll never know, not only from the money angle, but because of the time devoted to us. Going to the shops, cooking, washing and all the housework must have been a tremendous strain, but it's what mums did in those days.

'I think he said he was going round George's,' said Davy, shovelling some haddock in his mouth. George Mitchell was Manny's best friend and they were always together so that did seem a likely place for him to be.

'OK, I tell you what, Mum,' I said. 'I'll go round to George's house and see if he's there or if he knows where he is.'

So off I trotted to George's house and when his dad answered the door, I said, 'Hello, Mr Mitchell, I was wondering if Manny was round here, because it's teatime and he's wanted back at home.'

A frown came over Mr Mitchell's face and he said, 'No, he's not here. As a matter of fact, I was just about to come round to your house to see if George is there. We haven't seen him since just after school.'

Now this was a bit worrying. Where on earth could they be? We decided to go out and search for them. So we went off in different directions to look. After about half an hour without any luck I returned to the Mitchells' house to see if there was any news. About two minutes after I arrived, Mr Mitchell returned carrying Manny on his back, with George trotting by his side.

'They're safe,' Mr Mitchell said, putting Manny down. 'I found them in Bethnal Green Road. They were sitting on the kerb but I had to carry Manny back. He couldn't walk any further because he said his wooden toe was hurting him.' I did a double take. Manny put his finger to his lips, signalling to me to keep shtum.

I thanked Mr Mitchell and together Manny and I left for home. As we walked back, I said, 'What was that all about your wooden toe hurting?'

Manny laughed, 'I know, what a *schlemiel*, eh?'

It was round about this time that we acquired our first radiogram, so saying goodbye to our old horned gramophone. It had never worked properly, if the spring didn't break, then governors would or the speed regulator would run too slow or too fast. How someone of my now impeccable taste in music put up with it I can't imagine, so I put quite a bit of my earnings towards our new acquisition.

With my new-found love for classical music I would be found at the corner of Cygnet Street and Bacon Street every Sunday morning as this was where about half a dozen record stalls were to be found, all selling second-hand records. Many of these records were compilation records or 'Gems' as they were called, so you'd get *Gems from The Geisha*, *Gems from Chu Chin Chow* or, more generally, *Gems from the Operas*. Sometimes there were *Selections from…*, which were exactly the same sort of record. With my vast operatic knowledge I was always on the look-out for names on the record label, such as Caruso, Melba, Chaliapin and, of course, Alfred Piccaver. Before parting with my threepence, I would examine the record carefully for scratches and marks, looking at it from all angles with the eye of one who knew what he was looking for. Sadly, multiple scratches were all too prevalent on the *Gems from...* records on that corner.

One of the reasons I was able to put some money to the radiogram was because I finished my apprenticeship and Sam asked me if I'd like to stay on and work for him as a fully-fledged woodcarver for 1/6d per hour, which meant that my pay just about tripled from the top apprenticeship rate I had been on, though even then, I knew that the going rate for an experienced carver was 1s. 9d. an hour, even 2 shillings for those known to be the best in the business. I accepted his offer, although it was in my mind to eventually leave and try my hand at other shops to gain more experience. In fact I received an offer straight away from another local carver, Ephie Cohen, but I thought it would be a bit unfair to up and leave Sam as soon as I was out of my apprenticeship and give him the problem of finding a new carver after he'd spent five years training me. I didn't want to hurt him in this underhand way especially as Ephie was one of our customers. So I decided to give it at least six months before looking for another job.

George Clancy had poached a couple of our customers since setting up in business on his own by undercutting Sam's prices. It was not in my nature though to do this sort of thing. I never told Sam about Ephie's offer. As it happened, Ephie went broke about six months later and went off to manage the Golden Key Furniture Company in Old Ford. The owner of the Golden Key was a man called Lubelsky, who started out in Columbia Road in a small shop and prospered with his speciality, which was bedroom suites. They kept about six carvers in regular employment.

A new boy was taken on at about this time, a ginger-headed lad from Hoxton, known to all of us as Weasel. He was not apprenticed.

Although I didn't leave Sam, I decided it would be good to get a bit more experience of different types of woods and different types of carving so when Sid Longcroft, a darts buddy of mine, asked me if I'd like to do a bit of work for him, I jumped at the chance. His was a longstanding business which he had taken over from his father many years before. His speciality was mahogany dining tables, the big, heavy kind with claw and ball legs and acanthus leaves on the knees. I chose to do piecework for him because I could earn more that way and come and go as I pleased, within reason.

Because we were now working together, Sid and I teamed up as a darts pair and, after work, visited the two local pubs, the Royal Oak in Columbia Road, just a few doors down from Sid's shop, and the Birdcage. We challenged all comers in these two pubs, with the losing pair expected to buy the drinks, usually a half-pint of ale. Invariably we used to end up with a row of glasses of beer on the counter. Sid would give them a good pasting, but I always gave mine away as I was not a great drinker, perhaps two halves all night.

After staying with Sam and doing a bit of work for Sid for about six months, I came to the definite decision that now was the right time for me to move on. As luck would have it I happened to bump into Ephie Cohen again quite by chance. He told me there was a job going at Lubelsky's with the added information that the foreman, Bill Burchall, was not too well and might be leaving soon. He felt sure that I was good enough to take his place. So, after handing in my notice to both Sam and Sid, I finally made my way off the manor for the first time taking my first-ever bus journey to work. The number eight bus took me from Brick Lane to the Lady Franklin at Old Ford. It was summer time and the factory was surrounded by greenery, probably just weeds, but to me it was a wonderful sight, just like working in the country. I loved it there.

The work was very easy after Joe's heavy tables, just small carvings and frets. As it happened I found Bill Burchall to be in rude health and very robust, no sign of the illness that was just about to carry him off. Still, I forgave him as he turned out to be a very nice helpful geezer, putting me at my ease and explaining my part in the grand scheme of things.

I really enjoyed working at Lubelsky's until the mornings and evenings started to get unsociable, dark, rainy and foggy. Oh yes, fog was a real hazard and in real peasoupers you could lose your way completely. Old Ford took on a completely different aspect and I decided it was time for pastures new. I gave in my notice and was off again.

I was now about to indulge in a bit of law-breaking. I signed on at the Labour Exchange, thus getting 10 shillings per week unemployment pay, but I went to work part-time for Sid and George again. As nobody of our class paid income tax, it made this little caper easy. My only problem would come if they sent me after a job, but, as luck would have it, they didn't. At first I only signed on for six weeks because anyone staying out of work for longer than that was called up before a Court of Referees to be interrogated as to why they hadn't found work. I then went to work part-time in a factory in East Road, Hoxton and part-time for a firm in Columbia Road called Davenport's. The foreman there was a man called Charlie Deeks, who I believe was the uncle of John Deeks, the father of the famous *Carry On* and *EastEnders* actress, Barbara Windsor, who caused a scandal by leaving his wife, Barbara's mother, to live with and eventually marry another woman. That other woman was none other than Aunt Carrie's daughter, my cousin Julia. Though all this was still some time in the future when I worked at Davenport's.

After a few weeks working at these two places, I left and signed on unemployed for six weeks again, while working for Sid and George. Then I'd go back (officially) to East Road and Davenport's for a while, before signing off again and starting the whole cycle again. This lasted some time before I felt it was getting a bit dangerous and the Court of Referees might catch up with me.

It was then I decided that I really needed to settle down to a job and look for some sort of settled career before launching out into my own business which had always been my long-term plan. I found my ideal job with Steele Brothers in Scrutton Street, a turning off Curtain Road, the hub of the furniture trade. Their speciality was bedroom suites and I was the only carver employed. My initial pay was 1s. 9d. per week, rising to 2 shillings by the time my King and Country called on my services to beat the Hun. To the firm's everlasting credit, they sent me a couple of food parcels when I first went

233

into the army and they solemnly vowed to keep my job safe
for me until my return.

CHAPTER TWENTY-TWO

DEPRESSION, BATTLE OF CABLE STREET AND ABDICATION, 1935–6

'There is no poverty in the Soviet Union!'

Every Sunday morning, the local Communist Party used to hold a public meeting on the pavement outside the Salmon and Ball pub, on the corner of Cambridge Heath Road and Bethnal Green Road. Their secretary and main speaker, a man called Joe Vaughan, would continue somewhat in this vein, 'Workers live good lives there in comfortable homes with good clothes and without worrying about where the next meal is coming from. And you know why? Because they have a Communist Government that looks after them. There is no inequality in the Soviet Union unlike in this country where the rich get richer and the poor get poorer.'

He didn't have it all his own way though as the crowd was full of hecklers and a lively shouting match would take place so that Joe's eulogy and acclamation of the Soviet Union as a Heaven on Earth would provoke responses such as, 'Well, why don't you go and fuckin' well live there then?'

I suppose the difficulties suffered by me and my family as I was growing up and then brought home to me even more forcibly when I was sent out into the cruel hard world of work at the ripe old age of fourteen made me think more about politics. My childhood days were behind me as they were for all my friends and for all working-class children my age everywhere. And it was a cruel hard world for many. I was lucky as I was guaranteed full employment for my first five years, albeit on a low wage, but many weren't and had to find little jobs where they could or rely on hand-outs where they couldn't. England was in the grip of a punishing depression and the poster hoardings, as well as telling us to buy Andrews Liver Salts, were also urging us to 'Buy British'. Getting and keeping a worthwhile job was no easy matter. Millions were unemployed and living in the sort of dire straits our family knew only too well.

Poverty under the Labour Prime Minister, Ramsay MacDonald, was just the same as it was under the Conservative, Stanley Baldwin. The disillusioned poor had expected a better type of poverty.

The Communist Party tried to exploit this state of affairs, holding numerous meetings on street corners and in school halls. In their opinion, their leader, Harry Pollitt, was just the man to give us the best sort of poverty. By the age of about fifteen or sixteen I began to think more about politics as I tried to make some sense of it all. Until then I had assumed that the reason some people were very rich while some people were very poor was just an inevitable fact of life. But now I began to ask myself why some people were so poor whereas other people were so very rich. I knew that Mum and Dad were both staunch Labour supporters and always voted this way. Indeed, this continued until the grim reaper struck them off the electoral roll many years later.

Although I still had seven long years to wait before I would get my chance to vote, I decided to find out as much as I could about why there was such inequality and how it could be overcome, so, as well as going to the Salmon and Ball on most Sundays, I started going to the political meetings that were held on a regular basis in Rochelle Street School. I can remember one meeting there when the Communist Party's local candidate for MP, Dr Dunstan, was ably supported by a man rejoicing in the name of Shapurji Saklatvala who had come up from Battersea. I was very impressed by what Saklatvala said and the way he said it. I later discovered that he was, in fact, one of the very few Communists ever elected to the UK Parliament.

But it wasn't just the Communist Party who were trying to exploit this sad state of affairs as the rise of Fascism confirmed. Over in Europe, men like Hitler and Mussolini had risen to power on the backs of this poverty, promising to alleviate the suffering of their countrymen and help them lead healthy and wealthy lives. They had become dictators and now there was a political movement in Britain, the British Union of Fascists, trying to emulate their success, with a former Labour politician called Oswald Mosley at their head trying to become Britain's Führer or Duce.

But the Blackshirts, as Mosley's followers were called because they were prone to dress up in a quasi-military uniform with their black shirts being the most prominent feature, were not content with just holding meetings on street corners and in church or school halls, though they did that as well, but they took to marching through the streets intimidating with threats of physical violence anyone who stood up to them and tried to oppose them. And, on many occasions, not just threats but actual bodily violence.

They had decided, as Hitler had done in Germany, that immigrants, in particular the Jews, were to blame for all the country's ills, pointing to rich Jewish bankers like the Rothschilds and the Montagus, overlooking the fact that well over 90 per cent of all Jews in this country lived in abject poverty, particularly in the East End of London, which was Mosley's main target. At first, Mosley's propaganda gained some success and he had a big following amongst the non-Jewish working class of the East End.

The mid-1930s became a very scary time for us Jews living around Bethnal Green and Whitechapel as the Blackshirts began to randomly attack Jews on the streets and smash the windows of Jewish shops. It was very unwise to go out on your own, especially after dark, so we normally hung around in threes or fours, came home from the pub together and so on. Mum and Dad were continually warning us not to go out alone and, above all, to make sure Julie was kept safe. They were worried sick about what some of those vile Blackshirt bastards might do to her if they caught her alone. So we never let Julie go out anywhere on her own. We'd go with her to work and take her out to meet her friends and make sure we were there when she wanted to come home. There was a very intimidating and menacing atmosphere abroad at the time and, as Jews, we knew we were the number one targets.

Along with Jewish groups, the Communist Party, the Labour Party and the Trade Unions began to organise to try to stop Mosley and his kind and scuffles broke out at various meetings.

This division in our society in those uneasy days led to a number of individuals finding themselves in serious family dilemmas. Bob Gadston, for example, who was captain of our darts team, was the eldest of three brothers. His youngest brother, Archie, was very much to the left in politics, while the middle brother, known universally as 'Nutty', was a Blackshirt. As for Bob himself, he wasn't very political but he married a Jewess and Nutty vowed never to speak to him again.

Then there was Danny Betts, the boy whose father took that fatal dose of Lysol. He joined the Fascists, while his younger brother was a Communist. They used to row and fight all day and night.

Although I didn't like the idea of getting involved in fights, I knew that this could be a matter of life and death for us. If the Blackshirts ever gained power, who knew what our fate would be? It didn't bear thinking about, so I supported the Jewish organisations in their attempts to stop the Fascists on the streets.

The epitome of this struggle between the two sides came at the famous Battle of Cable Street on Sunday 4 October 1936, when I was twenty years old. The Blackshirts planned a march to go through Aldgate and Whitechapel in the very heart of our Jewish community. Posters were pasted up everywhere proclaiming the march, with the added information that it was to go through the 'Jew-ridden and communistic' streets of East London. It was intended to be a march of triumph for Mosley and his Fascists to show they now owned the streets of East London.

On the Saturday, I met up with a few of my mates in the Royal Oak and we discussed the following day's march.

'We gotta get down there and stop 'im,' was very much Percy Bates's opinion. Teddy Payne was not so sure, 'There's going to be a lot of trouble. A lot of fighting.' 'Scared, are you, Teddy?' Percy came back at him, 'What do you think, Alf?' I had been pondering this very question for some days now. My view was that both were right. Mosley and his Blackshirt thugs had to be stopped, we couldn't go on living in this atmosphere of fear, but there would be a lot of fighting and I didn't know if I was brave enough to get involved. Just a short while before, they had held a rally at Olympia in West London, where several hecklers got in. Those poor bastards were severely beaten up by the Blackshirt thugs and most finished up in hospital with serious injuries.

After a sip on my half-pint, I finally said, 'I guess Percy is right, he has to be stopped. But I can't see anything wrong in Teddy being scared about what might happen. There's going to be a lot of fighting and we might well get hurt. But it's nothing compared to what'll happen to us if Mosley is allowed through and starts lording it over the East End. Just look at what's happening to Jews in Germany. We've already seen Jewish shops smashed up over here. Percy's right. He has to be stopped.'

'So, you're gonna come along tomorrow, Alf?' Percy asked.

'Yes,' I replied, having more or less backed myself into a corner over it.

'Ok, this is the plan,' Getting to his feet, Percy announced, seemingly to the whole pub. 'The bastards have announced they're gonna try and march through the East End and us bastards are gonna make sure they don't. The *Daily Worker*'s printed a map of where the cunts are marching tomorrow and have asked us all to meet up round Gardiner's Corner at the junction of Whitechapel Road and Commercial Road as well as nearby Leman Street and Cable Street to stop them.'

It was obvious that even if the numbers turning out to oppose the march caused some last-minute change of plans and route, the occupation of Gardiner's Corner would be vital as that was the hub of the area and whatever route the Blackshirts finally took would have to include Gardiner's Corner.

'They're due to start at 'alf past two,' Percy continued, 'but we need to get there very early to ensure they can't start at all. So, we're meeting up at eight o'clock by the Bandstand and going off together from there. Now, one more pint everyone and get 'ome and get yourselves ready. Try and find something at 'ome you can break a Blackshirt's skull open with, even if it's only a rolling pin. The time has come to stop that wanker Mosley and his bastard Blackshirts, once and for all.'

Percy sat down to a big round of applause and shouts of 'We're with you, Percy!' Personally, I never knew Percy had it in him. I'd known him for many years, and although I knew he was to the left in politics, I had never heard him make a speech like this or organise anything like this before.

When I got home that evening I was very quiet. In spite of telling Percy I would be there, I was still unsure and thinking about what I should do the next day. Should I stand up against the Fascists or was it going to be too dangerous? Mum noticed I wasn't my usual lively self and said, 'What's wrong, Alf? You seem a bit quiet.'

I hesitated over answering as I didn't want to worry Mum and Dad, but it was Dad who broke the silence, saying, in his usual very perceptive way, 'Are you worried about tomorrow and the Blackshirts march?' I nodded.

'I don't think they'll be coming round this way,' he said. 'In any case, we'll just stay indoors.'

'No, it's not that exactly, Dad,' I began. But was interrupted by Mum, who broke in with, 'You're not thinking of bloody well going out and confronting them, are you?'

I nodded my head again, but this time more assertively, and said, 'We have to stand up to them, Mum, otherwise things will just get worse. If they're not stopped, they'll just carry on beating up Jews in the street and smashing our shop fronts in. Look how worried you are about Julie. We can't just let that go on. We can't live our lives in continual fear.'

'Oh, and you're going to stop them, are you?' she replied.

'Not on my own, of course not, but there will be thousands of Jews out there on the streets and I just feel it would be wrong to duck out of it and rely on them to win our fight for us.'

She sat silently for a while and then said, almost tearfully, 'But, Alf, it's going to be dangerous out there on the streets. Mosley and his mob are thugs and they'll think nothing of caving your head in if they get hold of you.'

I shrugged. 'But that's why we have to do it, Mum, and why I have to do it.'

For the first time since starting the conversation, Dad chimed in. He had been sitting listening to us and taking it all in. Finally, he said, 'Alf, I am so proud of you,' then took a more than unusually long drag on his cigarette before getting up and going outside.

Mum gave me a long hard look and finally said, 'Well, I can't stop you, Alf, if you're really determined. But just do one thing for me.'

'Sure, Mum,' I replied. 'What's that?'

'Don't let Davy or Bill or any of the others go with you. One broken skull in the family's bad enough,' she said.

'OK, Mum.'

I didn't get much sleep that night, so the following morning I was awake early and got ready to go out. I decided not to take any weapons with me, not even a rolling pin, as my idea was to try to stay out of trouble as much as possible and hang around in the background, but at least be there to show my support. As agreed I met up with Percy and a few others at the Bandstand. 'Good to see you,' Percy announced to those who had turned up. 'Now let's go and knock the livin' daylights out of those Fascist cunts.' And with that, he started off with the rest of us following.

We set off down Brick Lane towards Gardiner's Corner. As we passed Fashion Street, back on my old manor of Spitalfields, I began to hear a lot of noise coming from further down the road, which grew louder and louder as we got nearer. All around us there were other people walking and running in the same direction, some with clubs or pickaxe handles, some even with the full pickaxe. By the time we reached Wentworth Street, I could see hundreds, maybe thousands, of people further down the road. The march was due to take place at half-past two and it was not yet 8.30, but already the turnout of anti-Fascists was far greater than I had expected.

On reaching Whitechapel Road I was amazed by the number of people thronging the area. There were barricades all along the street, made up mostly of timber from local woodyards. There were also many trade union, Labour Party and Communist Party banners being proudly held aloft as their members marched down the road to join the mass of people now occupying the road. The chants 'They Shall Not Pass' and 'Down with Fascism' had already started. Looking round at the scene and the people and the banners, it occurred to me that many of the people here protesting and doing what they could to prevent the Fascists marching were not Jewish, although there were many from my ancestral race there as well of course, but it gave me a great deal of heart and comfort to know that we were not alone and that ordinary English and Irish working-class people were prepared to fight alongside us to end the provocation, violence and hatred brought about by Mosley and his evil crew.

Looking towards Gardiner's Corner itself I could see hundreds of mounted police lining up, facing this growing crowd in Whitechapel Road. By this time there were people everywhere and our little group had been swallowed up and I lost contact with them, so I decided to cut down Adler Street to see what was going on in Commercial Road, which, we had been told, was the other main road Mosley might march down. It was exactly the same story there. Thousands of chanting people, barricades and banners with mounted police lined up facing them.

As the day wore on, more and more demonstrators arrived and more barricades were erected. Some tram drivers even abandoned their trams in the middle of the road so they too could be used to prevent the Fascists marching.

At about midday or thereabouts I heard a lot of shouting and screaming, even more than the general hubbub that was going on. It turned out that the police had charged into the demonstrators down both Whitechapel Road and Commercial Road in an attempt to clear a path for Mosley. I could see in the distance that police horses were charging repeatedly at the crowd, but there seemed to be very little movement as the lines held firm.

Suddenly, I heard a voice behind me: 'Alfie!' I turned round and saw my old friend Hymie Marcovitch whom I hadn't seen for some years. 'You come 'ere for a punch-up too?' he said. 'Well, follow me, nuffin's gonna 'appen down 'ere. That cunt Mosley won't be able to get down 'ere, there's too many of us. Even the police won't be able to clear a way for 'im. I tell you where the best place is, it's down Cable Street. You mark my words, that's where they'll try and clear a way for 'im, down Leman Street and on to Cable Street, there's less people down there.' As it happened, the last thing on my mind was to get involved in a punch-up, I was still hoping to stay well back from any fighting, but I followed Hymie as he nipped down Back Church Lane to Cable Street.

When we arrived there, it seemed there were hardly any fewer people down there either. Cable Street was filled with chanting demonstrators, just like Whitechapel Road and Commercial Road. There were more barricades, including one with an overturned lorry. People were busy ripping up paving stones with their pickaxes to throw on the barricades.

The street was also strewn with broken glass and marbles as a defence against possible mounted police charges such as were happening at Gardiner's Corner.

The whole atmosphere was so tense and electric. I had never known anything like it and although I was still hoping to keep out of trouble I was beginning to feel caught up in the pressure and feeling that I really did want to get at those bastards who had been trying to destroy our community. There was also a feeling of safety in numbers as there were far more demonstrators here than I had ever imagined there would be. It seemed like the whole of the East End had turned out to stop the Blackshirts.

By about one o'clock, the whole area was seething with people all intent on one thing, to make good the chant, 'They shall not pass!' At about this time I saw a mass of police at the top of Cable Street, not on horseback but trying to march in on foot, clearing away the barricades. 'I told you,' said Hymie, 'This is it. They're clearing out the street to let Mosley pass. Those bastards are as bad as the Fascists. They're not on our side, Alfie.' As the police started to march down Cable Street, not only were they confronted by the massed ranks of demonstrators on the street but from above as the people living in the flats over the shops hurled all sorts of things out of their windows on their heads, including many chamber pots full of urine and worse.

The police were unable to move very far and after a short while I saw them back up and turn round, marching back the way they came. From my vantage point some way down Cable Street I heard a tremendous cheer go up from the front. 'What d'you think's 'appened?' I asked Hymie.

'I think it could be over, Alfie,' he replied, dancing a little jig. 'They've given up. We've won, Alfie, we've won.' He threw his arms round me and gave me a very tight hug. 'We've fucked the bastards!'

And so it turned out. The police had been unable to clear a route for Mosley thanks to the sheer number and determination of the demonstrators and they'd ordered Mosely to call off his march. A great feeling of elation swept over everyone, me included. We danced in the street, hugging each other and chanting, 'They did not pass!'

News quickly spread that there was to be a victory celebration in nearby Victoria Park. Hymie headed off there but I decided not to go as I felt Mum and Dad would be worried sick about me, so I headed for home to give them the good news. When I walked in through the door, Mum threw her arms round me as though it was the first time she had seen me in years. 'I'm OK, Mum, I said. I didn't get involved in any fighting.'

'Thank God,' she said.

'What's happened, Alf?' Dad asked.

'We won, Dad,' I replied. 'We stopped the bastards marching.'

'Watch your language, Alfie,' Mum said quickly, and then hugged me again with a big smile on her face.

Although there were still a few more isolated outbreaks of violence from Blackshirt thugs against the Jewish community, the worst was over now and the Public Order Act which came into force the following year and banned the wearing of political uniforms while marching, saw to it that there would never again be any marches planned like this one. Blackshirt numbers fell dramatically, as many of them had only been in the organisation because they liked dressing up in uniform and marching. We had definitely turned the tide at Cable Street and I was proud to have played a part, however small, in it.

The year 1936 saw another big national crisis play out. This time involving the Monarchy. The year previously, 1935, Sonning Buildings had paid homage to its beloved monarch, George V, on his silver jubilee. Bunting was hung between the two trees in the playground and from upstairs windows to the same two trees. Some people displayed flags, others portraits of their well-loved King and Queen in their windows. A children's party was held beneath the bunting while the adults toasted the King's good health, mainly from pint glasses. Songs were sung including one calling upon God to bless the Prince of Wales as well.

Less than a year later, despite the many toasts drunk to his good health, the King passed on to that special throne in Heaven's royal apartments.

Following the royal demise came the goings-on of the former Prince of Wales, now of course the new monarch, Edward VIII, and Mrs Wallis Simpson. She was a divorcee and therefore felt unsuited by the Establishment to be a Royal Consort. And so, despite all our entreaties to God to bless this noble person, he turned his royal back on us and left the country with his beloved Wallis, as he had decided he couldn't 'discharge my duties as King as I would wish to do without the help and support of the woman I love'. We were now kingless as his proposed coronation turned into an abdication instead.

In its hour of need, the country turned to the abdicated king's brother, the Duke of York, to take on this onerous job. After all, no one likes to feel kingless. When he accepted there was great rejoicing throughout the land, especially in May 1937 when he became the official new king upon his coronation.

CHAPTER TWENTY-THREE

LOVE AND MARRIAGE,
1937–9

With many of us now reaching adulthood plus a new baby girl, the council in its wisdom once more decided that we were living in overcrowded conditions and moved us yet again, this time to a flat in Marlow Buildings which had an extra bedroom. It was also quite unusual in that it was a two-storey flat with a staircase in the front room leading to three bedrooms upstairs. The fourth bedroom was reached through a door off the living room. It was all fully self-contained with water and a sink in the kitchen and our very own inside lavatory.

The only drawback was that it was another top-floor flat. There were never any half measures with us, we were either on the top floor or the ground floor. So, it was another job for the piano people while we did all the rest of the moving ourselves.

We were living in uncertain times with the rise of Nazi

Germany on the continent and a few months later, sometime in the summer of 1937, Percy Bates, still staunchly anti-Fascist and with the smell of victory in his nostrils after Cable Street, announced to a surprised Teddy and me in the Royal Oak that he was going to join the army.

'I've given it some thought,' he said, 'and I've decided to sign up.' We both looked at him without saying anything until Teddy finally managed to say, 'Whatever for?'

'There's going to be a war sooner or later,' Percy replied, 'you mark my words.'

Teddy looked doubtful and responded with 'I don't think so, Percy. Chamberlain seems convinced that there isn't going to be a war and that he can do business with Hitler.' (Neville Chamberlain had recently been elected Prime Minister.)

'Chamberlain's a schmuck, Teddy,' said Percy dismissively, 'and you shouldn't be one too.'

I had some sympathy with this point of view and said, 'You may be right, Percy, but surely it's a bit too early to say definitely.'

'Hitler's a mad man, nuffink and no one is gonna stop him till he's conquered Europe and killed all us Jews, especially not that idiot, Chamberlain. We'll 'ave to do it ourselves by force. There will be a war and that's all there is to it. 'Ave you thought about signing up, Alfie?'

'I can't say it had ever really crossed my mind, Percy,' I replied. In truth I had a lot of sympathy with Percy's point of view but I had no desire to move away from home at the moment just as I had settled down with a good job and reasonable pay.

'Well I'm going,' Percy finally said. 'In fact I'm goin' down the recruitment office tomorrow.' And with that our conversation turned to its more normal topics of sport and girls.

Percy was as good as his word and, after a week or so, was sent away for training. A couple of months later he came home for his first spell of leave resplendent in his new uniform. He looked quite changed, so smart and full of his new way of life. Teddy and I met him for a drink in the pub and he spent all evening recommending the joys of army life as heartily as any recruiting sergeant might have done. In spite of our previous conversation, Teddy in particular was very impressed and told Percy he would seriously consider the matter. I once again declined his kind offer. That next day, Teddy talked it over with his mother, but because she was unhappy about his going, especially as her husband, Teddy's father, was dead and she didn't want to be left on her own, he decided against it. Although I didn't know it at the time, his mother's feelings on the matter were crucial to my future life and happiness.

A couple of days after Percy went back to the army, Teddy and I arranged to go out for the evening, so I went across to Moorgate, where he worked as a foreman in a furrier's, to meet him when he left off work. This was the first time I had ever been to his workplace. As I waited for Teddy to emerge from the front door, I saw this really stunning young girl walk out. She had a very attractive face with blonde hair and delicate light blue eyes that seemed to hide a sadness behind their sparkling appearance. She was quite tall and elegant with a gorgeous figure. I was smitten immediately but was too tongue-tied to say anything to her. Teddy was not far behind her, so I said to him, 'Who's that girl? What's her name?' He smiled and said, 'That's Joyce Sinnott. She's a bit of all right, eh, Alfie?' I nodded. 'I've been thinking of asking her out myself,' he added. That is not what I wanted to hear but I let the matter drop and we went on to take on all comers at darts in a local pub, thus ensuring free drinks for the evening.

I couldn't get Joyce out of my mind, but I wasn't sure what to do, so it was with some surprise that a couple of days later I heard Teddy say to me, 'Oh, Alf, what about coming out on a double date with me? I've arranged to take that Joyce Sinnott and her friend Doris out on Saturday. I said that you'd come.' Now I wasn't too pleased at the thought of Teddy being with Joyce while I was with this unknown quantity, Doris, but I thought it might give me a chance to get to know Joyce better, so I said, 'Yeh, OK. Sounds like it might be fun.'

So, on Saturday, Teddy and I went over to Rotherhithe, which was where Joyce and Doris lived. We just went for a walk but halfway through the evening Doris got fed up and went home because nobody was taking any notice of her. The reason for this being that both Ted and I were paying so much attention to Joyce. But I was pleased to see that Joyce seemed to be more interested in me than she was in Teddy and after a while Ted must have noticed too because he said, 'I think it best if I just left you two together.' He then said 'Goodbye,' and walked off. Joyce and I walked around a bit more until I took her home.

As we got to her door, she said, 'Thank you for a lovely evening, Alf. You'd better not come in though, my dad won't like it. Let's say goodbye here.'

I nodded and said, 'It's been a wonderful evening for me too.'

Then, as she turned the handle on the door, I plucked up the courage to say, 'Joyce, can I see you again?' She turned and said, 'Of course,' before pushing the door open and going in.

I was on cloud nine. Now this seemed to me like the real thing and nothing at all like how I'd felt with Percy's sister Sophie.

I thought hard about where I could take her on our first proper date. As it happened I had seen a big poster advertising all-in wrestling in New Cross. I thought this would be the ideal way to start our courtship, especially as the stars that particular night were Norman the Butcher and the Giant Anaconda, two giants of the ring. Sadly, Joyce did not agree and, as soon as the first bout started, she jumped up from her seat and ran out. The delicate art of this cultured sport was entirely lost on her. It cost me a shilling as well.

Fortunately this did not put her off me, though I thought it prudent to keep away from boxing, cricket and football matches when with her. Girls want some understanding! And so, the pictures and walks, arm-in-arm with me always taking the side of the pavement nearest to the road as was the custom of the time, became the main feature of our courtship. We also visited each other's homes, though that was more often to my home than hers, mainly because her workplace was fairly near, so she would come over for dinner after work and spend some time there before I took her to her home via a walk through Rotherhithe Tunnel. Sometimes, but not by any means every time, I would call in for what they called supper, but was in fact just a cup of cocoa made with water and a spoonful of condensed milk.

But there was another reason why we spent more time in my flat apart from it being handy to pop into after work. And that was because of her father. Her mother was a very nice person and made me feel very welcome. I think the best that could be said for her father was that he tolerated us and didn't really say much to me. But I could see right from the start that he was very nasty to her mother. If the family – Joyce had three sisters and two brothers, though one wasn't living at home – were awaiting his arrival home from work, the atmosphere was one of fear and a feeling not unlike that portrayed in *The Barretts of Wimpole Street*. He was a thickset man and an ex-sailor who worked for the Port of London Authority as a lock keeper in the nearby Surrey Commercial Docks.

Before we went to her house for the first time, Joyce explained to me the reason why there was only one brother living at home. This was because her father had thrown her brother Bill out of the house when he tried to prevent him from striking her mum and refused to let him back in again. He was only eleven at the time and he had to go and live with a friend of their mum's until he got married ten years later. She told me that her father often hit her mum and sometimes hurt her very badly. I think drink played a very large part in his uncivilised behaviour.

As bad as he was, he seemed very fond of Joyce, but because of the way he treated her mum, she felt only hatred towards him. To me, this state of affairs was definitely a new experience. Dad was undoubtedly the chief in our house, but no one was afraid of him and it would certainly never have crossed his mind ever to strike Mum. Compared to Bill Sinnott, he was an absolute angel.

The more we saw of each other the further the distance between Rotherhithe and Shoreditch seemed to grow and many's the night, through lingering a little longer with Joyce, I would miss the last 47 bus and have to walk home. So one Friday night, several months after we'd started going out as we were walking home from the pictures through Southwark Park, I said, 'Let's sit down' and I guided her to a park bench. 'I want to ask you something,' I said as I placed my arm round her shoulders. Joyce didn't respond, so I carried on, 'I've been thinking about us and how much I love you, Joyce. And I hope you feel the same about me.' She gave me a smile. 'You know I do, Alf,' she replied. I paused a bit then said, 'Joyce, I think we ought to get married. What do you think?'

She didn't reply straight away and I thought maybe I had made a big mistake in asking her. Eventually she looked into my eyes and said, 'Alfie, you know I love you and yes, I want to marry you more than anything in the world, but I'm really worried about my mum. I can't just up and leave her with that wretched man.'

I didn't know what to think. I was overwhelmed that she wanted to marry me but this was tempered with disappointment at the idea that she couldn't contemplate leaving her mother for me.

'I tell you what,' I said eventually, 'why don't we get engaged and see how things go? There's no rush. Let's give it another year and hopefully in that time we can sort out some other arrangements for your mum.'

Joyce nodded. 'Yes, Alfie, let's do that.' We sealed the deal on the bench with a long kiss and cuddle.

The following day I bought her a cheap – very cheap – engagement ring with a promise to get her a better one later. A promise I nobly fulfilled a few months later when we were walking down the Old Kent Road one Saturday afternoon, heading for the Trocette, a cinema in Tower Bridge Road. We happened to pass a jeweller's shop and we looked in the window. I said to Joyce, 'Pick out a nice engagement ring that you like.' She did and I went in and bought it for her. It cost six guineas. A few days later, Joyce returned the compliment by buying me a ring in Deptford High Street. The following week, her mum threw a small engagement party for us. It all seemed to be getting very official now, what with proper rings and a party but we still hadn't set a date as we were still in a quandary over Joyce's mum.

As the party was coming to an end, however, her mum took us both to one side and said, 'Look, I know you've been putting off the wedding day for my sake. Although Joyce hasn't said so in so many words I know that's the reason you haven't named the day. Please don't worry about me. My husband's caused me nothing but grief since we've been married, but I don't want him to ruin your lives as well. Please, for my sake, don't let the bastard get away with that as well. I'll be all right. I've lasted this long and you can always come and visit me to make sure I'm OK. In any case Sally and Jim – ' Joyce's youngest sister and brother – 'are both still at home. They'll look after me.'

So, after the exchange of rings and the party and Joyce's mum's kind words, the time had come to seriously think about getting married and setting a date. We finally took the plunge eleven months after we said we would give it a year, deciding to get married on 2 June 1939.

Our engagement and proposed marriage meant that for the first time a member of my family would be marrying outside the Jewish race and faith. It made no difference to me. I loved Joyce and that was that as far as I was concerned. I couldn't care less what race and religion she came from. Mum and Dad, Julie and all my brothers were happy for me and it didn't matter to them either. But I know there were some mutterings around the Buildings about this state of affairs. To the more *frum*, the idea of a Jewish man going out with a goy was unthinkable, actually getting married to her was even worse, and I did begin to get the cold shoulder from a few people. Although I was by no means the first Jew to do this, it was nevertheless a change to the accepted order and it was the older generation particularly who found it difficult to accept. By the late 1930s though it was beginning to happen more and more and I think ours was really the first generation where this began to become acceptable as a more or less normal part of life. Some of my friends married gentiles and in our family, eventually both Julie and Davy married out of the Jewish religion and, many years later, so did Manny.

However, things did not go as smoothly as we had hoped as about a week or so before the wedding was due to take place, Joyce was taken into Guy's Hospital, suffering from a bad kidney infection. The hospital's treatment was to give her sticks of barley sugar and plenty of water.

Fortunately, the hospital agreed to let her out for the wedding but said she had to go straight back in afterwards as apparently she needed more barley sugar. So we got married in Bethnal Green Registry Office on the appointed day and, after going back to my flat for our wedding breakfast, which consisted of a cup of tea and a lump of Mum's bread pudding, Joyce went back to hospital. Spending our wedding night apart was not the start I had planned for our wedding and, I strongly suspected and hoped, neither had Joyce!

A few days later she came out and we moved in to our first place together, two rented rooms in a house in Culling Road, a turning off Jamaica Road in Bermondsey. It was a first-floor flat, all self-contained. We called the owner of the house Mole. I have forgotten why, unless his name was Mr Mole or maybe he used to go burrowing in the garden. The location suited us fine as it was only a few minutes' walk from Joyce's house in Albion Street, so we could look in on her mum regularly.

Mum and Dad bought a bedroom suite for us. It cost £13 and we are still using it to this day! They also bought us all our pots and pans, while Joyce's mum gave us a canteen of cutlery. Aunt Sarah gave us two large figures with mirrors on them, Davy and his fiancée Connie, gave us an eight-day chiming clock and Bill gave us a lovely pink glass vase standing in a pink glass bowl. We also bought ourselves two elephant-shaped ornaments in Woolworth's, then a 3d and 6d store. Talking of Davy and Connie, they too got married, about three or four months after we did.

On the first Sunday after we moved in we held our own little celebration and splashed out on a nice piece of beef for dinner. But it wasn't just the moving in together we were celebrating as Joyce had had some news of her own for me. When the hospital said she could go home, I had gone up to meet her and bring her back. As we left the hospital, she said, 'Can we go for a cup of tea first, Alf, I have something to tell you.' This worried me a bit as I thought it might be something to do with what they had found was wrong with her in hospital. But, although it was something to do with what the hospital had told her, it wasn't bad news at all. Quite the reverse in fact.

'Alf,' she said as she sipped her tea, 'the doctors did lots of tests on me while I was in and . . .' she hesitated, '. . . they found I was expecting.' I was gobsmacked. 'I had a feeling I was, but they confirmed it,' she went on.

At first I couldn't say anything, and, funnily enough, the first thing that came into my mind was a memory of that day in Palmer Street, now long ago, when Uncle Woolfy told us that Aunt Betsy was expecting and I had no idea what he was talking about. Now though I knew what the word expecting meant all right, and all sorts of thoughts flashed through my head. As I took the news in, I held Joyce's hand across the table and just said, 'Joyce, that's wonderful.' She gave me a big smile and nodded. 'When's it due?' I finally asked.

'They said I was about two months gone, so it'll be some time in the New Year.'

'We'll have to celebrate,' I said as the news continued to sink further in.

'Not just yet, Alf,' she replied, 'I'm still a bit tired from the hospital.'

'Of course, of course,' I said. I think it was at that point that it finally hit home, because I jumped up from our table and shouted out to everyone in the café, 'I'm going to be a dad!'

They all looked at me, while Joyce, dying of embarrassment, buried her head in her cup of tea.

'Congratulations, mate', said one old boy in the corner, while other people held their cups up to us in a sort of toast. 'Can we go?' Joyce muttered.

When we left we went straight round to Joyce's mum to tell her the good news and then over to see my mum and dad to tell them. Mum was overwhelmed. She even broke out the best china – oh yes, we now had some proper china cups bought from a stall down the Lane at a halfpenny each, such was our growing affluence with Julie, me and my brothers all out at work, not just broken jam jars – and made us a cup of tea with a piece of leftover bread pudding from our wedding day feast. 'Alfie, Joyce,' Mum said beaming, 'I should be so lucky to be a *bubba*. Thank you. You've made me so happy.' Dad put in, 'Congratulations both of you, now you can find out what we've suffered all these years!' Mum gave him a look but he just shrugged his shoulders and said, 'What?'

Julie and the others all chorused their congratulations and best wishes. Davy added, 'You do realise you've made Clara an auntie at the age of five?' We all laughed. Clara, who hadn't really taken much part in all of this, looked up and said, 'But aunties are all old women.' And we all laughed again.

So our first Sunday lunch of roast beef turned into a double celebration for us but there was a small downside to the celebration. There was some beef left over, so Joyce put it back in the oven, supposedly for another day. We didn't have any fridges then of course. We used to keep our milk and butter or marge cool by standing them in a dish or saucepan of cold water. As it happened, we forgot all about the piece of meat in the oven and it must have been a week later when Joyce opened the oven and saw the meat running alive with maggots. I wrapped it up in newspaper and Joyce took it over to her mum, who buried it in her garden.

Although we celebrated that first Sunday with a splendid roast beef dinner with all the trimmings, our normal Sunday fare was still lokshen soup, which was down to me to make as Joyce had never had it before meeting me and didn't really know the 'secret' of how to make it in the good old Jewish tradition, or was it just my Mum's tradition? So a Sunday roast was still not quite the norm but we were able to afford beef or pork for dinner something like once a month or so because we had both come a long way since our poverty-stricken younger days as children in large families and, although we weren't rich by any means, we both had good jobs with a relatively healthy income and, as yet, no children to spend it on but with the good news that one was on its way to make our little family complete.

And so we were very happy and felt we had everything to look forward to and that our futures looked very rosy if only there wasn't such a very large cloud on the horizon that was about to engulf not just our happiness but everyone else's throughout the country.

CHAPTER TWENTY-FOUR

FEAR, WAR AND BIRTH OF FIRST CHILD, 1938–40

Although the threat to our individual safety from Blackshirts out on the street was now more or less a thing of the past, there were other, greater things to worry about. Neville 'peace in our time' Chamberlain had replaced Stanley Baldwin as Prime Minister in 1937 and gathered around him a group of notorious appeasers, amongst whom, and sticking out like sore thumbs, were John Simon, Lord Halifax, Neville Henderson and Samuel Hoare. People who really thought that if only they could teach Hitler how to play cricket he would give up all his territorial demands and keep within his own boundaries. Churchill thought otherwise, along with Lord Vansittart, Duff Cooper and Anthony Eden. History has long since confirmed who was right in this little disagreement. Hitler never got his name into Wisden's and Chamberlain was run out early in the war, leaving Churchill to take guard on a very sticky wicket.

And so throughout the time of our courtship and the early days of our marriage, we were living in very uncertain times. Chamberlain started his toing and froing to meet Herr Hitler, appease would probably be the right word, convinced that he could do business with this monster. Nevertheless, in spite of Chamberlain's optimism, the nation was urged to take up some sort of National Service in case war did break out. Leaflets and booklets were published, especially on air raid precautions. Even cigarette cards were issued on the subject. Air raids were the fear uppermost in most people's minds after seeing the terror, death and destruction wrought on Spain during the Spanish Civil War by the Fascist aircraft on all the cinema newsreels.

After the euphoria of September 1938, when the piece of paper in Chamberlain's hand, which he waved on his arrival back from Munich, told us the fear of war was banished for ever, it soon became obvious to all except Chamberlain's most devoted followers, who unfortunately formed the majority of the government, that the Führer's antics meant war was not only not banished but was more or less inevitable. The job of recruiting air raid wardens, war reserve policeman, and the ATS (Auxiliary Territorial Service) amongst many other similar occupations went into overdrive as they were signed up in large numbers, while 1939 saw National Service introduced for young men.

London began preparing for the inevitable as trenches were dug out in the big parks, sand bags in their thousands were stacked around most public buildings and hotels, restaurants, places of entertainment, factories, and even some private houses placed stirrup pumps and buckets of sand in key places ready to deal with any incendiary bombs that fell, which, if left unattended, could cause terrible fires. Windows began to be criss-crossed with sticky paper to prevent bomb blasts showering glass all over the show.

In the Buildings, many ground-floor flats were taken over for conversion to air raid shelters with the ceilings being shored up to give them extra strength. In the street brick shelters were constructed along with deep brick reservoirs which would be filled with water to help the firefighters. The Auxiliary Fire Service started to appear in our area, comprised of taxi cabs pulling a fire pump behind.

George Bradshaw, who lived in Marlow Buildings, was appointed our ARP (Air Raid Precautions) warden. He was a veteran of the Mesopotamian campaign in the First World War. When the war came, his job was to see that all lights were blacked out, especially in the flats, and to guide people to the shelters in an air raid. All shelters displayed a big 'S' to help locate them. We had our very own War Reserve Policeman as Dad volunteered for this arduous job, having had experience of a similar role in the First World War. He underwent his training in Old Street Police Station. We used to joke in the family that if Hitler saw him undergoing his training he would double his bet.

Further preparations for the inevitable included the issuing of gas masks and the drawing-up of plans to evacuate children and pregnant women.

Everyone, including us, knew the storm was about to break

whatever Neville Chamberlain said. Those war clouds were getting ominously close. The newspapers and wireless were always full of the latest threat to people and telling us how to act in an emergency. As a Jew I felt doubly threatened, and as dismal as the future now appeared, I knew in my heart that this war had to be fought. Not only was Hitler threatening to rampage all over Europe but he was also threatening to completely eliminate all Jews from the face of the earth. I could not stand by and allow others to fight my fight for me.

By the end of August 1939, when Hitler invaded Poland, everyone knew the time had arrived and the planned evacuation programme was put into operation with young children and pregnant women being shipped out of the big towns into the country. One of those to be given her orders to leave was Joyce, by now about five months' pregnant. She was told to report to Victoria Station, where she was to meet a group of women and children going down to the south coast, to Eastbourne. I went with her to the station and there, amid the kisses and the tears, we said our farewells, with the promise that I would come and visit her every weekend and more often if possible.

The German invasion of Poland made war inevitable as she had received a guarantee from Britain and France that they would come to her aid if she was ever violated by Germany. Even now though, in spite of this blatant act of aggression and disregard for international law and treaties, Chamberlain was reluctant to honour this obligation and continued to insist that we should talk to Herr Hitler. Eventually he was forced by Parliament to send an ultimatum to the evil man of Europe to withdraw his forces, or else. The ultimatum expired at 9 a.m. on 3 September. With no answer being received, we found ourselves once again during the lifetime of many people, including me, at war with Germany.

As soon as Joyce was evacuated, I moved out of our house in Bermondsey back to Mum and Dad's, so I was in their flat in Marlow Buildings when we tuned in to the wireless at 11.15 a.m. on Sunday 3 September to hear Chamberlain say, 'This morning the British Ambassador in Berlin handed the German Government a final note stating that, unless we heard from them by eleven o'clock that they were prepared at once to withdraw their troops from Poland, a state of war would exist between us. I have to tell you now that no such undertaking has been received, and that consequently this country is at war with Germany.'

It had finally happened. The moment we all feared and dreaded but knew was inevitable was now upon us. We all felt scared but in some way relieved. Mum started crying and was comforted by Dad. Manny was the first to speak and said, 'About time too! I'm gonna sign up tomorrow. I'm gonna get that bastard, 'Itler, and sort 'im out once and for all.' For the only time I can remember, neither Mum nor Dad remonstrated with one of their children over their use of bad language. In fact, we all fell silent after this outburst, each of us wrapped up alone in our own private thoughts about what this war was going to mean for us. The silence was shattered a few minutes later when the first air-raid warning of the war was sounded. This was much more frightening than the practice ones we had become used to. This was real. And there's no getting away from it, nor any polite way of putting, we were all shit-scared. As we had planned, we all quickly went down to the flat below, with Dad carrying Clara. Looking back on it, I'm not really sure why we had said we would do this as it was just as vulnerable as ours, but down we went, were welcomed in by the occupants, Tommy and Freda Stern, and waited. For what we did not know. Perhaps the worst, gas, bombs, fire, ruins. Who knew? After what seemed like a lifetime the all-clear sounded. It was probably no more than a quarter of an hour. But here we all were unscathed and very relieved and thanking our hosts. We trooped back upstairs, shaken but safe.

People started to come out of their flats talking about this first incident of the war. Bill, Abie and I went to see George Bradshaw to get his opinion of the event and to see if he knew what exactly had happened. At the entrance to his block, Mike and Annie Phillips, who lived on the ground floor with their two children, were holding an inquest.

Annie proudly pointed up to the barrage balloons and said, 'They can't get through those. They'll keep the bastards out.' Mike shook his head mournfully and replied, 'There's no gates up there, Annie.' An answer that in the months to come was to prove all too true.

For the time being though, no more sirens were heard. This period was what was later to be called the 'Phoney War'. There were no bombs, no more air-raid warnings and very little happened on the western front. We tuned into the news on the wireless every night and every night we heard the same story, 'The French are surrounding Saarbrücken.'

On the home front, Dad was helping to maintain law and order while Abie got a job with Miller's, a big importer of

American comics and pulps. They also printed and published their own versions of the comics but in black and white. Abie worked in their warehouse in Hackney Road. However, he didn't stay long as he decided that the comic business was no joke and he left to find a job at a tailor's, where he became apprenticed to that fine art.

Mum must have been a very worried woman at this time. A war just starting and her with six sons, all young men of eligible age to join the army (or nearly, as Manny would soon be sixteen). I wonder how many sleepless nights she had. Though as it turned out, not all of us went into the armed forces. Only four of us eventually made the grade. Although Manny had sworn to join the army 'to show 'Itler' the day after war was declared, he had to wait until he was eighteen in 1942. As soon as he was he applied to join, without waiting to be conscripted. The rest of us waited till we received our call-up papers – we were in no rush.

After Abie, Bill, Manny and I had all signed up, it was Joe's turn to go along to the recruiting office following receipt of his call-up papers. He was asked by the recruiting sergeant if he had any brothers in the army. He replied he had four, so the sergeant said, 'Four brothers in the army? Don't you think your poor mother must be suffering enough?' With that he gave Joe a green card, a medical exemption, meaning he was not fit enough to join the armed forces. The reason given was severe myopia. Though his short-sightedness wasn't nearly as bad as Bill's, who was passed fit and assigned to the Auxiliary Military Pioneer Corps. Davy was also turned down on medical grounds, on account of the damage to his legs caused by the road accident he had when he was young. However, all of this was still in the future as none of us had yet joined up and Mum still had us all at home.

After a month or so of the phoney war, on one of my regular visits to see Joyce in Eastbourne, she said she would like to come home again as nothing much seemed to be happening. I was absolutely delighted and we came back the same day, moving into our flat in the Buildings. But as this made it too overcrowded and gave us very little privacy, we soon found a place of our own, two rooms above an empty shop in Redchurch Street, which was fairly near the Buildings in the notorious former Nichol area. Although the shop below was now empty, it was once the café where most of the neighbourhood ne'er-do-wells used to meet and no doubt plan their latest piece of villainy.

Above us lived a mother and her daughter. Both us and them had to go up a narrow wooden staircase to get to our rooms. If ever there was a fire trap, that house was it. In a corner of one room, which we used as the kitchen, there was a shallow oblong brown sink with just one cold water tap. Our bedroom looked out on to Lipton's tea factory (where Joyce went to work many years later). The rent was 7s. 6d. a week.

Once we had settled in, life carried on almost as in peacetime. Cinemas and other places of entertainment began opening up again. I was able to take advantage of this relaxation of the rules to see my first Gilbert & Sullivan opera. Although it was only a film and not the real thing, it was a good second-best to me. This was at the Odeon in Hackney Road and the film was *The Mikado*, starring Kenny Baker as Nanki-Poo. To Joyce's everlasting credit she sat through it all, no running out this time, which goes to prove that G&S is better than all-in wrestling. The only real reminder at this time that we were actually at war were the many barrage balloons in the sky watching over us like guardian angels, and the blackout.

As the nights started to close in on us, it began to get more difficult to get about. There was no street lighting and only very small glimmers from passing traffic making it very dangerous to be out and about on dark moonless nights. Torches were very hard to come by because batteries were almost non-existent. So to help Joyce and me get about I broke up a high-tension battery used in a wireless set, which released lots of smaller batteries. These batteries I put in a box. I then linked the batteries to a small bulb with a length of wire and we had our own home-made torch with which we were able to walk about the streets at night. I used to hold the box and Joyce would hold the bulb. To my family this was known as 'Alfie and Joyce's Contraption'. They thought it was a huge joke every time they saw us with it and someone only had to mention our Contraption to set them off roaring with laughter. But it did its job and we were able to beat the blackout to some extent. Although we were able to get around locally, visiting Joyce's mum in the evening was a bit of a step too far, so we confined our visits to weekends.

'Alf,' said Joyce one morning in January in the depths of the winter with some snow swirling around outside, 'it's time.' I knew what that meant, so we got ready to go to Mrs Levy's Nursing Home, a mainly Jewish maternity hospital, though all creeds were catered for. We looked in on Mum and Dad on our way to tell them they were about to be grandparents and then quickly crossed the railway bridge in Hare Street, arriving at about midday. John was eventually born about six hours later, weighing 7 lb 2 oz and Joyce and I became the proud parents of a baby boy. In the good old Jewish tradition of naming the first child after one of the father's parents depending on the sex of the baby, the name had already been agreed on. So that's how we already knew his name was John. What a time, though, for a child to enter the world – just as it had gone raving mad – but this too was in keeping with tradition, for, just like his father, he was born in the second year of a world war.

It was a cold, hard, freezing winter; coal was difficult to come by and not long after John was born the pipes froze in our flat, so we had no water. Bill used to bring us pails of water from the Buildings to keep us going. Somehow we managed to struggle through, and as spring came, the weather eased up and the nights began to get a bit lighter.

But the hard winter and lack of water was nothing compared to the blow that was about to befall us as one morning in April the letter we had all been anticipating and fearing arrived in that dreaded OHMS buff envelope. It was my invitation to attend an army medical board in Tottenham. I obliged and was passed B2, because of a varicose vein in my left leg. It was this that probably kept me out of the infantry, instead being allocated to the Royal Artillery. A short time after this I received another buff envelope telling me to report to Norton Manor Royal Barracks on 16 May. A railway warrant was enclosed.

On the assigned morning, I held John in my arms as I said my farewells to him before leaving him in the care of Mum while Joyce and I made our mournful way to the station. The shrill whistling of the guard as he waved his green flag came all too soon. Saying my final farewells to Joyce chilled my very heart. With misty eyes we waved to each other as the train began to slowly move forward. I suddenly realised the war had at last caught up with me and was now wrenching me away from my loved ones as it had already done to many thousands of others. Carrying on waving from out of the window as the train gathered momentum I saw her gradually disappearing into the distance before finally evaporating altogether as the platform was lost to sight. In the midst of a crowded compartment, I felt alone, lost.

The fear, apprehension and sadness of knowing you have to leave those you love and go off into the unknown is indescribable. That my two boys have never had it thrust upon them is the greatest blessing of my life, and perhaps the minuscule part I played in the Second World War helped. I like to think so.

AFTERWORD

I hope my attempt at bringing to life my father's description of his life and times is a fitting testament to him and what he and his family had to go through just to survive through the poverty and momentous world events that blighted his generation.

I feel that in many ways the worst thing that happened was that he was forced to leave school at fourteen – well, perhaps not forced exactly, but that the family's poverty meant there was never any choice in the matter. He loved English Literature and History and I think the way he spoke to me about his memories and the historical events of the time he lived through shows what heights he might have been able to achieve had he been allowed to study longer. Could he have gone to university? We will never know, of course. Not that there was anything wrong with the profession he did follow all his life. He became a master craftsman woodcarver, much in demand by some of the biggest furniture companies in the country later in his life, but there was never any choice in the matter. I'm not saying he was unique in this. Far from it, in fact. It was the lot of a whole generation before the war and it was very rare for any working-class child to escape the inevitable and stay on at school to 'better' him or herself.

As it turned out, financially he didn't do too badly after the war because furniture was much needed to replace that lost in the bombing raids or through the building of new houses to accommodate young families and clear away the slums of the past, so he and his family never again faced the sort of abject poverty he was subject to in the 1920s and 1930s. Even his dad was able to find steady work as a French polisher and with the family growing up and leaving home, his parents too lived a fairly comfortable life especially after being moved out by the council to a brand-new estate in the leafy suburbs of Chingford Hatch.

So, just to fill in briefly the story of Ikey/Alf's life from his going into the army to his return to Spitalfields in the 1990s: he spent five years in the Royal Artillery through the war. He would be the first to admit he didn't see a lot of action, being stationed mostly in Taunton and Clacton-on-Sea. He went across to Belgium and Holland several months after D-Day, when those two countries were securely back in Allied hands and his job was to help resettle families displaced by the Nazi occupation.

He was discharged from the army in September 1945 and

went to work for a large furniture company in the East End called Brooks' Furniture in Roman Road, Bethnal Green. After a year or so, he finally achieved his ambition of setting up in business on his own, taking on his old friend, George Clancy, to work with him in his shop in Columbia Road, Bethnal Green, a stone's thrown from the Buildings and Virginia Road School. By this time, however, he, Joyce and John had moved to a prefab in Hackney, courtesy of the LCC (London County Council), which meant a three-mile bus commute to work.

Alf's family was completed when I came along in May 1947. Much of our lives in the prefab in Hackney was the subject of my previous book, *Pie 'n' Mash & Prefabs*, which covers the period 1947–1965, when we were again moved on, this time by the LCC's successor, the GLC (Greater London Council), to a two-bedroom terraced house on the Debden Estate in Loughton in Essex. By this time my big brother John had moved out and was married, having graduated from Cambridge University, a place Alf could never have dreamt of going even in his wildest dreams. And yet here, just one generation later, his son had been able to achieve what had been impossible just twenty years previously, such was the rate of social change that had happened in the late 1940s and 1950s.

The move to Loughton meant that Alf now became almost a long-distance commuter, catching the Underground every day to and from work.

With the increasing prosperity, he was able to take Joyce and me on holidays abroad. The idea that even Southend was too far away and too exotic to even consider as a holiday destination was now turned on its head as it now seemed far too close, and over the years we had holidays in France, Austria, Italy, Yugoslavia and even the Soviet Union.

In the mid-1970s, Tower Hamlets Council, which now incorporated Bethnal Green, put forward a plan to develop Columbia Road and the surrounding area by building some new blocks of flats. Alf's workshop became a casualty of this plan as part of it involved the demolition of a number of shops including his. He was offered alternative accommodation, amazingly in Cleeve Workshops, where he had his first job at the age of eleven with Isaac Belancoff, the milkman, all those years ago. For Alf the wheel had come full circle and he finished his working life in 1981 in the same workshops as he had started it in 1927, fifty-four years earlier.

After his retirement he and Joyce moved for one last time, this time to a retirement bungalow in Clacton-on-Sea owned by the GLC. There they led a very active life, helping to look after my children, their grandchildren, and spending much time walking into town and down to the beach, a walk of some 40 minutes each way. It was on one of their walks into town that Alf saw, outside the offices of a coach company, a poster advertising a day trip to 'The Famous Petticoat Lane' and he made up his mind to take this nostalgic trip back in time, a trip which led to the outpouring of memories that formed this book.

And it was here in his retirement that Alf was at last able to indulge his passion for English Literature and History. He read voraciously and also turned his hand to writing, having several articles published in various magazines and journals such as *Picture Postcard Monthly*, *East London Record* and *Cockney*

Ancestor. He even wrote a novel set around the Bandstand just before the Second World War. One of the articles he wrote was about his memories and feelings of his last days at work:

> I had to break the news of my retirement to my customers, a very sad business this. Leslie Dvorkin in particular had been with me over thirty years ever since he started his small cabinet-making business after finishing National Service. He was more a friend than a customer. I said goodbye to all the neighbouring tradesmen in the yard, they in their turn wishing me all the best in my retirement. I gave my two work benches to Dave Plunkett, a carver friend of mine, who had his shop at no. 11 Marlow Workshops, just a staircase away from nos. 7 and 8, where, as a young lad of fourteen, I had set out in earnest on the long road to senior citizenship and pension book.
>
> To me the day I started seemed like only yesterday. In that time the once mainly Jewish shops had all but disappeared with new waves of immigrants taking their place. What to me seemed like strange fruits and vegetables began appearing in the markets, mainly to appeal to this new wave of West Indian and Asian immigrants. I imagine that was how much of our culture had appeared to the English when the Jews first began to settle the area with our lokshen, challah, beigels, gefilte fish, matzos, latkas and the rest.
>
> Virginia Road School, despite all the changes taking place around it, still stood its ground as an institute of

learning, although judging by the teachers I saw making their way into that establishment, I felt pretty sure that the Messrs Wiggins and Barnett type of teacher, resplendent in their three-piece suits, collars and ties, had long since gone, banished into history.

But now the day of departure had finally come as I prepared to hand in the keys to my workshop to the local GLC office, ending a working life that had begun, when a schoolboy, with Isaac Bellancoff's milk round, from these very same workshops which I now locked up for the final time.

So it was now goodbye to the area I had been reluctantly brought to from my home in Palmer Street some fifty-five years previously. Goodbye to the once teeming Jewish life that had brought such warmth and respectability. Goodbye to the Buildings. Goodbye to the now almost deserted Bandstand, once the playground of the young, the hub of local life and the political forum of the old. And finally goodbye to all the ghosts of my boyhood and youth still forever real in my memory.

What had I achieved in those fifty years, I often asked myself. Well, apart from the war years, I had stood at a bench all my working life, having been brought up to believe that regular work was a luxury in itself and that if you were able to pay your way and keep out of debt you could sleep safely at night. Well, at least I had been able to achieve that and keep my family safe and fed. All in all I have had a good life and I look back on it with great contentment.'

AFTERWORD

Alf passed away on 27 January 1999 in Clacton Hospital at the age of eighty-three, having suffered a severe stroke a few days earlier. He was surrounded by his loving family, Joyce, John, me and his two devoted grandchildren, Robert and Tom.

GLOSSARY OF YIDDISH TERMS

The definitions of the words are generally specific to the context in which they are used in this book: other definitions apply elsewhere; spellings are many and varied. A number of the expressions are not very polite: insults, along with the food, were enthusiastically embraced and utilised by the largely English-speaking population of the East End.

alte kaker   old shitbag

beigel   a ring-shaped bread roll, boiled before baking; it is much better known by its spelling bagel, but the Kosher Kingdom blog (http://kosherkingdom.tumblr.com/post/47619936837/bagel-or-beigel)

suggests a difference between the two: the
beigel, it argues, is 'the granddaddy of the
bagel'; the latter is 'the big business, multi-
grained, poppy-seeded, gluten-free, sugar-
free, brown, white, wholemeal, chocolate,
cinnamon and any other flavour you can
think of, bagel, we know and love today'.
The traditional beigel, however, is made by
hand, using old recipes, none are identical
and they do not come in a huge variety of
flavours.

bubba   grandmother

bubbeleh   dearie, darling

dreck   rubbish, crap (literally and figuratively)

drerd   [from (*in*) *der erd*, '(in) the ground'], under
the ground, Hell; *Ikh hob dir in drerd*:
literally 'I have you in Hell'

fleish   meat

frum   religious, Orthodox

gonif   thief

goy   a non-Jewish person

lokshen	noodles
mazel tov	congratulations
momzer	good-for-nothing, bastard
nafka	slut
narrishkeit	foolishness, nonsense
nebbish	useless creature, weakling, a nobody
oy gevalt	exclamation of alarm, dismay (similar to *oy vey!*)
platzel	Jewish white bread roll made with onion
Pullock	Polish immigrant (possibly a variant of 'Polack'), here used dismissively of the Polish Jews who were comparative latecomers to the UK, but not intended as racist slurs
putz	fool, jerk (in the impolite sense)
schlemiel	idiot, dupe
schlorem	knick-knack
schmaltz	excessive sentimentality

schmuck   irritating person, fool, jerk, tool (in the impolite sense)

schnorrer   beggar, parasite

schtick   pattern, routine (act), gimmick, area of expertise or interest - 'thing'; also, to laugh

shadkhen   matchmaker

shtum   quiet

shul   synagogue

tuches   buttocks

yenta   busybody (formerly 'gentlewoman')

yentz   screw, fornicate

yok   non-Jew (derogatory)